The New York African Burial Ground
Unearthing the African Presence in Colonial New York

HOWARD UNIVERSITY PRESS
Washington, D.C.
2009
Published in Association with the General Services Administration

Acknowledgments and Credits

The *New York African Burial Ground: Unearthing the African Presence in Colonial New York* is a publication of Howard University's New York African Burial Ground Project. The information in this book is derived primarily from Volumes 1, 2, and 3 of the series of the same title. The titles and editors of those volumes are: *Volume 1: The Skeletal Biology of the New York African Burial Ground,* edited by Michael L. Blakey and Lesley M. Rankin-Hill; *Volume 2: The Archaeology of the New York African Burial Ground,* edited by Warren Perry, Barbara Bianco, and Jean Howson; and *Volume 3: Historical Perspectives of the New York African Burial Ground,* edited by Edna Greene Medford.

Any opinions, findings, and conclusions expressed in this publication do not necessarily reflect the views of the U.S. General Services Administration or Howard University.

Published by Howard University Press
2225 Georgia Avenue, NW
Washington, DC. 20059

ISBN: 978-0-88258-259-7
0-88258-259-3

Howard University's African Burial Ground Project was funded by the U.S. General Services Administration under Contract No. GS-02P-93-CUC-0071.

Publication Preparation
Michael Heilen and Maria Molina (Statistical Research), and Brian Fagan (Lindbriar Corporation)

Graphics Support
Margaret Robbins (Statistical Research)

Design and Layout
Simpson and Convent

Cover Design
Star Bullock + Associates, Mark A. Bartley

Cover Images
Detail of Maerschalk Plan (Frances Maerschalk, 1754)
Burial 335 (photograph by Dennis Seckler)
African Burial Ground National Monument (U.S. General Services Administration, Carol M. Highsmith Photography, Inc.)
Artifacts from the New York African Burial Ground (photographs by Jon Abbott)
     Enamel cuff link face, Burial 371, Catalog No. 1875-B.001
     Bead Type 12, Catalog No. 01651-B.79
     Ring, copper alloy with glass insets, Burial 310, Catalog No. 1486-B.001
     Bead Type 15, Burial 340, Catalog No. 01651-B.75
     Cast silver pendant, Burial 254, Catalog No. 1243-B.001

$\mathcal{C}$ONTENTS

FOREWORD

Long forgotten and once remote, New York's African Burial Ground was the final resting place of hundreds, possibly thousands, of people of African descent who lived and died in New York in the seventeenth and eighteenth centuries. It is located in what is now the bustling financial district of Lower Manhattan.

The New York African Burial Ground: Unearthing the African Presence in Colonial New York briefly tells the story of the rediscovery and recovery of that site and of its importance to the city, state, and nation. It is a complex and captivating story involving many people, places, cultures, and concepts over many centuries and across many continents.

Ultimately, the New York African Burial Ground represents triumph over adversity and victory over extreme challenge and circumstance. Its story unfolds now, in the twenty-first century, only through the tireless efforts of many dedicated community members, public servants, civil servants, scientists, and historians who spoke up, lobbied, investigated, and challenged each other to ensure that the people buried in that once-again sacred space receive their just recognition and respect. The General Services Administration, on behalf of the American people, provided funding for several initiatives related to the New York African Burial Ground Project.

The content of this book is derived primarily from the three reports that form the foundation of Howard University's New York African Burial Ground Project—*The Skeletal Biology of the New York African Burial Ground, The Archaeology of the New York African Burial Ground,* and *Historical Perspectives of the New York African Burial Ground.* Prepared to be easily accessible by the general public, the purpose of this book is to explain in layman's terms, project activities and research findings. To that end, it provides an overview of the massive research project whose goal was to study that site and "unearth" the depth and breadth of the African presence in New York. It briefly presents the findings resulting from the study of the unearthed bones and artifacts in scientific laboratories at Howard University, John Milner Associates, and other research centers where dozens of scientists and academics devoted countless hours to this project. It also explains key concepts and theories addressed by the researchers. Photographs, illustrations, maps, and charts mainly from the technical volumes, bring the substance of the researchers' explorations to life in vivid detail.

Many people have struggled to ensure that the story of the New York African Burial Ground is told, true and clear, and for a variety of audiences. We hope that this publication will help people from different backgrounds and experiences gain a better understanding of the importance of this site and of the involvement of African Americans in the birth and growth of New York and our nation as a whole. We encourage readers to delve deeper into the project research by consulting the aforementioned larger technical volumes.

O. Jackson Cole, Ph.D.
Howard University Executive-in-Charge of the African Burial Ground Project

James A. Donaldson, Ph.D.
Dean, College of Arts and Sciences
Howard University
Washington, D.C.
December 2009

The New York African Burial Ground

${\mathcal{T}}$HE AFRICAN BURIAL GROUND

CHAPTER 1

${\mathcal{I}}$n a remote part of colonial Manhattan that would later become the center of bustling New York City, African people, though enslaved, maintained their dignity by celebrating the links between the living and the dead at the African Burial Ground. In so doing, they made the plot of ground designated for their interment a deeply sacred place. We will probably never know the names and identities of the men, women, and children buried in the graveyard. By studying the bones and materials recovered from their burial ground, however, we now know much more about their lives. This is the story of the African Burial Ground and the people who were buried there.

The New York African Burial Ground Project

The New York African Burial Ground is one of the most important archaeological and historical discoveries of the twentieth century. The burial ground was first used actively around 1650 and was closed by 1795. Located in what we now know as Lower Manhattan, New York City, the burial ground was the final resting place for as many as 15,000 people. Most were enslaved Africans. Others were free Africans or people who had escaped slavery or indentured servitude. Research teams in the disciplines of history, archaeology, and skeletal biology joined together to study the remains of these African New Yorkers, whose burials are evidence that their hard work, varied skills, and diverse cultures built one of the world's great cities and contributed much to New York's history. Forgotten for more than a hundred years, part of the African Burial Ground was uncovered in 1991 during archaeological excavations at 290 Broadway. The site was excavated because the General Services Administration (GSA) agency needed to build federal offices there. At first, archaeologists thought that only a few burials, perhaps 50 at most, were present in some areas of the site. Most of the graves, they believed, had been destroyed by earlier construction on the site.

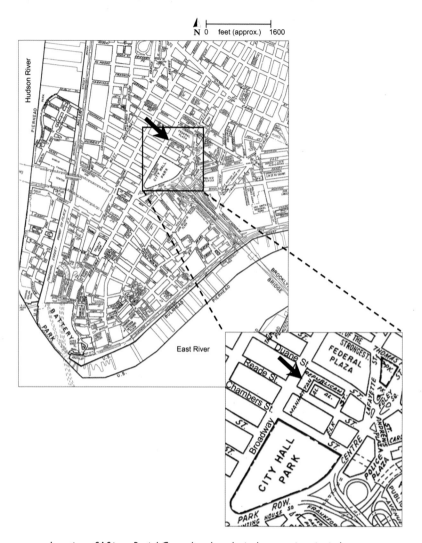

Location of African Burial Ground archaeological excavation site in lower Manhattan, New York. Arrows point to Block 154. New York City Mapped Streets, Section 12, 1997. (New York City Mapped Street: Section 12—Borough of Manhattan, New York County; used with permission of the New York City Department of City Planning. All rights reserved.) (From The Archaeology of the New York African Burial Ground, Part 1.)

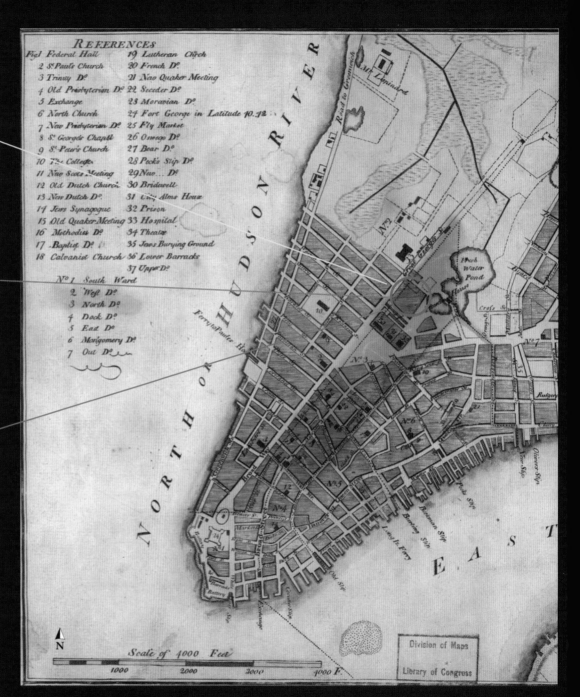

Top, *Burial 12 (from* The Skeletal Biology of the New York African Burial Ground, Part 2); middle, *enslaved domestic laborers in eighteenth-century New York (illustration by Michael Colbert, 2004) (from* Historical Perspectives of the African Burial Ground); bottom, *construction during archaeological fieldwork (photograph by Dennis Seckler);* right, *the Directory Plan of 1789, showing the city just before the closing of the African Burial Ground (Geography & Map Division, Library of Congress) (bottom and right images from* The Archaeology of the New York African Burial Ground, Part 1) .

The archaeologists were in for a big surprise. Soon after excavation began, a number of human bones were unearthed. Then, burials containing intact skeletons were found. Earlier construction had not destroyed the burials, because the burial ground had been covered by as much as 25 feet of dirt after the cemetery was closed in 1795. By the time the 1991–1992 excavation was completed, more than 400 burials had been found.

No one involved in the initial archaeological dig had anticipated such a find, and the GSA had not made adequate plans to treat the site and the human remains found there in a respectful and scientific manner. In addition, the concerns of the descendant community were not being considered by the GSA. As a result, the archaeologists were not equipped to do the job that was required. This lack of preparation meant that no research plan was developed to determine how to study the site or involve the public. The methods used for excavating the burials did not include recording all that was required to conduct a proper study of the people buried there. Important research questions were not asked. The appropriate ways to study the site were not in place. No plan was developed to memorialize the site or to rebury the remains. The laboratory facilities were not adequate for storing artifacts or human remains. In part, these problems came about because the archaeologists were not provided the time or materials to do the best job. Other problems arose because experts in African American archaeology, history, and skeletal biology had not been asked to become involved.

African American New Yorkers were outraged by how the project was being carried out. Public officials, archaeologists, and other members of the public were also very concerned. Many members of the public felt that the excavations were being done in a disrespectful manner and that the legal steps required to study the site had not been followed. Members of the community voiced concern over whether the burials were excavated correctly and whether the right information was collected. Some questioned why the burial ground was being excavated at all. They wanted the burial ground left alone. Others wanted the remains to be studied, so that African Americans could learn more about the history and contributions of those who came before them. Many blamed the GSA for these problems, but the archaeologists working on the site were blamed as well.

In response to this uproar, an expert in the study of skeletal biology, who was African American, was asked to be involved. He was Dr. Michael Blakey, then director of the W. Montague Cobb Skeletal Collection at Howard University. Dr. Blakey inspected the site and its laboratory and found many problems.
Along with public officials and many other archaeologists, he became involved in public meetings the GSA then convened to involve the public in the project.

Section 106 of the National Historic Preservation Act

The protection and management of many archaeological sites in the United States is made possible by Section 106 of the National Historic Preservation Act. Section 106 requires that archaeological sites be identified and evaluated for significance and integrity for projects on federal or public lands or involving federal or public funding. Sites that are considered significant, like the New York African Burial Ground, can be nominated for listing in the National Register of Historic Places. If a National Register site will be affected by a construction project, then these effects must be assessed. For the New York African Burial Ground Project, the GSA, the Advisory Council on Historic Preservation and the New York City Landmarks Preservation Commission developed an agreement that addressed the descendant community's concerns and established how GSA would address the impact of construction on the burial ground. The agreement resulted in the use of public funds to study the site, rebury the human remains, report on the findings, and provide access to the project materials and data at the Schomburg Center for Research in Black Culture, a division of the New York Public Library. The agreement also resulted in the creation of a documentary video and a memorial and visitor center at the site.

Backhoe clearing adjacent to temporary archaeological excavation shelter early in the fieldwork (photograph by Dennis Seckler) (from The Archaeology of the New York African Burial Ground, *Part 1).*

Descendant Community

A descendant community consists of those individuals who could have ancestors among the people who used or created an archaeological site. For the New York African Burial Ground Project, the descendant community consisted of African Americans living in New York City and many other areas around the country. Precisely who was buried in the burial ground or their genealogical relationship to living African Americans cannot be known. As a result, all African Americans have an equal stake in how the remains of these ancestors are to be treated and studied. Before the New York African Burial Ground Project, few descendants were included in the study of African American sites. Now, early and constant involvement of African American descendant communities is considered a necessary component of any project involving the excavation and study of African American sites.

Members of the descendant community were not initially included in planning the New York African Burial Ground Project. The concerns of this community were excluded and ignored at first. African Americans made their voices heard, however, and fought to have their concerns addressed. They did not all share the same opinions about what should be done when they discussed what the burial ground meant to them and what they felt needed to happen. Achieving consensus on the concerns and recommendations of the descendant community nonetheless became crucial to decisions made

Night procession of "The Ties That Bind" ceremony in November 1993. The event celebrated the transfer of remains from the excavated burials to Howard University in Washington, D.C., for study prior to their reinterment (photograph by Roy Lewis) (from The Skeletal Biology of the New York African Burial Ground, Part 1*).*

Egunfemi Adegbolola, Chief Alagba of New York, commemorating the ancestors in a Yoruba ceremony at the African Burial Ground (photograph by Dennis Seckler) (from The Archaeology of the New York African Burial

It soon became clear from these meetings that the public, particularly the African American descendant community, was deeply concerned.

Concern over the excavations reached such a high pitch that the United States Congress became involved. Congress held two subcommittee hearings in 1992 to decide what should be done. Late in 1991, the Advisory Council on Historic Preservation, the GSA, and the New York City Landmarks Preservation Commission had signed an agreement requiring the GSA to develop a plan for removing, studying, and reburying human remains from the site and for caring for data and research materials after the project was completed. The agreement also required plans for public involvement, the production of a documentary video, and the development of a memorial and interpretive center. The hearings revealed that the GSA had not fulfilled its legal responsibility with regard to the burial ground and that the terms of its agreement with other agencies were not being met. As a result, experts in African American studies from Howard University and archaeologists from John Milner Associates were chosen to write a plan for a comprehensive study of the site. Howard University is an institution of higher education with a long history of service to African Americans and other people of African descent. John Milner Associates is a company with archaeological expertise in studying African American burial grounds. Together, they would create a plan to learn about about the people who used the New York African Burial Ground and how and when they used it. The process would use knowledge from various disciplines and require experts in history, archaeology, and skeletal biology. Their research was to determine where the people buried at the site

Mayor David Dinkins (center), Peggy King Jorde (Mayor's Liaison), and Howard Dodson (Chief, Schomburg Center) (front) are briefed on the excavation in 1992 by Michael Parrington (Principal Archaeologist for HCI and John Milner Associates) (left) (from The Skeletal Biology of the New York African Burial Ground, *Part 1).*

Congressional Hearings on the African Burial Ground

On July 27, 1992, U.S. Representative Gus Savage convened a Subcommittee Hearing on the African Burial Ground. At the time, the archaeological study of the human remains lacked an appropriate research design, and the GSA was seen as not fulfilling its legal responsibility in running that study. After hearing testimony from archaeologists, historians, concerned citizens, and public officials, Savage concluded that the GSA was in violation of its legal responsibilities and interagency agreements. As a result of the hearing, excavation in the burial ground area was ended, and the New York African Burial Ground Project, an interdisciplinary research effort led by Howard University and John Milner Associates, was launched. A second hearing on September 24, 1992, checked on the progress of the project.

A Federal Steering Committee was created in October 1992 in response to the hearings. The committee resolved to: (1) establish a museum to commemorate the African Burial Ground as a national landmark, (2) erect a memorial within the landmark area, (3) develop signs interpreting the history and culture of Africans in the landmark area, (4) install and exhibit memorial artwork in the lobby of the office building, (5) rebury remains in excavation areas, and (6) accompany reburial with international, sacred ceremonies. All of these resolutions have been carried out. The resolution to establish a museum resulted in the establishment of the National Museum of African American History and Culture. Construction of the museum on a 5-acre site adjacent to the Washington Monument, in Washington, D.C., will begin in 2012. The GSA and the National Park Service expanded on these resolutions to designate the New York African Burial Ground as a National Monument. They established the African Burial Ground Visitor Center, with exhibits and education programs, within the lobby of 290 Broadway.

Lines of Evidence: Burial 147

Researchers examined skeletal, archaeological, and historical evidence to learn about the individuals buried at the New York African Burial Ground and to reconstruct who those persons might have been in life. For example, one of the oldest individuals in the excavated sample was found in Burial 147. By analyzing bones and teeth, researchers determined that the individual was an elderly man between 55 and 65 years old. The condition of his eye sockets, cranium, and the enamel of some of his teeth indicated poor nutrition or disease during his childhood. Infection or injury had affected his arm and leg bones, suggesting he had survived many hardships during his long life.

Between the man's chest and upper right arm, archaeologists found a cluster of small metal rings, and along his arm bone, a series of regularly spaced pins. The pins may have been used to enclose the rings in an armband, pouch, or sack pinned to the man's sleeve. The researchers suggest that the rings could have been part of a "conjuring bundle," which would have contained items to be used by the man's spirit to communicate with ancestor spirits. Historical research shows that hiding amulets and conjuring bundles on the body has been a practice in many African cultures for centuries, both in Africa and the Americas. At other African American sites, archaeologists have found similar bundles of pins, crystals, buttons, smooth stones, and other items thought to have been used as charms or conjuring items. Based on historical and archaeological evidence, the researchers concluded that the man in Burial 147 could have been a conjurer.

The placement of this burial in an area of the cemetery used during and after the Revolutionary War led researchers to determine that this elderly man was buried between 1776 and 1795. Given his advanced age, he may have lived in New York City for much of his life or been one of many African refugees who escaped to the city during the Revolutionary War.

Drawing of Burial 147, showing three pins aligned along the inside of the right upper arm (drawing by M. Schur).

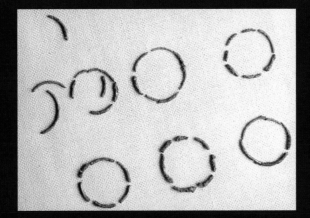

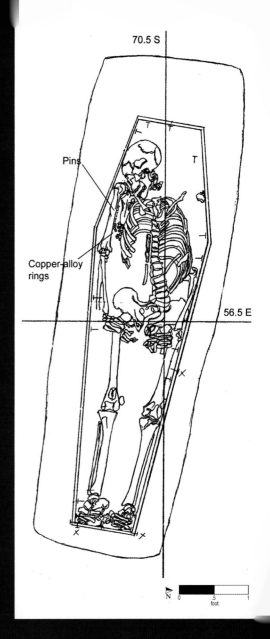

The complete drawing of Burial 147, including the coffin outline, site and grid lines, and locations of artifacts on different parts of the skeleton (drawing by M. Schur).

came from, how they arrived in New York, and what happened to them afterward. The research would examine how and when they lived and died and how they were buried. Because the people buried at the site came from different parts of Africa and from different cultures, the research needed to focus on African as well as New York history and culture. Many enslaved Africans were transported to the Caribbean before being shipped to New York, so the experience of enslaved Africans in the Caribbean needed to be studied as well.

After the second Congressional hearing, the 290 Broadway excavations were stopped, and no more archaeological work was allowed. Fifteen intact burials that had been exposed but not yet taken out of the ground were left in place and covered with clean fill. Further building and construction was not allowed on areas of the site that had not been excavated. Thus, the GSA was able to build only some of its planned structures. Congress stopped the rest. The more than 400 burials excavated up to that point formed the basis of the scientific study known today as the New York African Burial Ground Project.

Howard University and John Milner Associates were now directed to lead this research, which was supported by the GSA. Dr. Blakey was named Scientific Director of the project. He quickly put together a large team of scholars with expertise in history, archaeology, and skeletal biology to study the site. The results of their findings have been published in the series titled *The New York African Burial Ground: Unearthing the African Presence in Colonial New York.*

As a skeletal biologist, Dr. Blakey was also the Director of Skeletal Biology for the project. He and Dr. Lesley Rankin-Hill coedited Volume 1, *The Skeletal Biology of African Burial Ground.* Dr. Warren Perry was named Director of Archaeology. He coedited Volume 2, *The Archaeology of the New York African Burial Ground,* with Dr. Jean Howson and Dr. Barbara Bianco. Dr. Edna Greene Medford was named Director of History. She served as the volume editor for Volume 3 of this series, *Historical Perspectives of the African Burial Ground: New York Blacks and the Diaspora.*

The information and material presented in this book are based on the findings from Volumes 1–3. Please see the editors' profiles provided at the end of this volume, as well as lists of the many contributors who made Volumes 1–3 possible.

To educate the public about the New York African Burial Ground Project, the GSA established an Office of Public Education and Information in the World Trade Center in Lower Manhattan. Dr. Sherrill D. Wilson, an anthropologist with expert knowledge on the African presence in New York, headed this office, which reached out to more than a

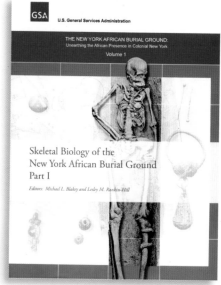

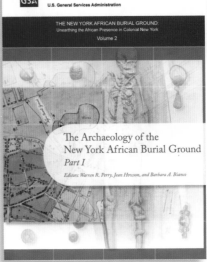

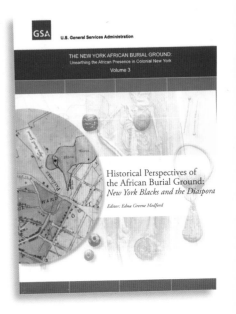

The three technical volumes that form part of the series: (from top to bottom) Volume 1, The Skeletal Biology of the New York African Burial Ground; *Volume 2,* The Archaeology of the New York African Burial Ground; *and Volume 3,* Historical Perspectives of the African Burial Ground: New York Blacks and the Diaspora.

Bioarchaeology

As Scientific Director and Director of the Skeletal Biology (or bioarchaeological) component for the New York African Burial Ground Project, Dr. Michael Blakey oversaw the study of bones and teeth from project site. Bioarchaeologists study human skeletons from archaeological sites to learn about the age, sex, growth, development, and death of individuals. Bioarchaeologists can also learn about origins, diet, cultural practices, and work by studying the skeletal remains. Many methods are used to learn about individuals by studying their remains; for instance, the opening of a woman's pelvis is wider than a man's to allow a baby to pass through the opening during childbirth. As a result, the shape of a mature pelvic bone can be used to determine whether an adult was a man or a woman. The stage of development of teeth and different bones in the body can be used to determine the age at which a person died. The effects of disease, nutrition, or injury on any given person can also be determined by examining abnormal changes to bones and teeth as well as evidence for healing after damage occurs. Studies of joints and places in the skeleton where muscles attach to bone allow bioarchaeologists to learn about the kinds of work people performed in the past. Isotopes and trace elements in bones and teeth can be used to learn where people were born, where they lived during their lives, and what kinds of food they ate. In combination with historical and archaeological information, information learned from studying the skeleton was used to learn about the health, economy, culture, and quality of life of people buried in the New York African Burial Ground.

Project Director Michael Blakey and Data Systems Manager Douglas Fuller discuss organization of the database (from The Skeletal Biology of the New York African Burial Ground, *Part 1).*

Osteological Technician Assistant Joseph Jones involved in cleaning and reconstruction (from The Skeletal Biology of the New York African Burial Ground, *Part 1).*

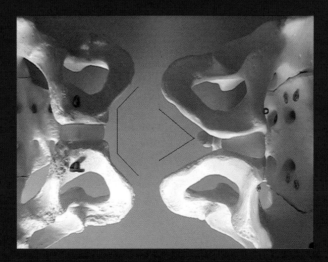

Comparative male and female pelvic shapes. Note the wide subpubic angle in the female (left) in relation to the male (right) (from The Skeletal Biology of the New York African Burial Ground, *Part 1).*

hundred thousand people, many of them African American students, to tell the story of the African Burial Ground and the people for whom it became a final resting place.

The Research

Howard University project scientists worked closely with the descendant community and a large team of researchers to decide what needed to be studied. Where did the people buried in the burial ground come from? Who were they and what were their backgrounds? What happened to them while they lived in New York? What were their lives like? How did they resist slavery? What aspects of their heritage did they retain? How did they see themselves? How did others see them? How did they change? Those were just some of the questions the researchers and the descendant community wanted answered by the study.

The researchers and the descendant community also had strong feelings about the terms used to refer to the people being studied. They wanted the people buried in the African Burial Ground to be called "enslaved Africans," not "slaves," because in their view, the word "slave" suggests that a person's identity is defined and limited by slavery. This was not the case for the Africans and African Americans who used the burial ground, they emphasized. Those people were forced into slavery, and the term "slave" defines only how Euroamericans saw them. As a result, the researchers adopted the term "enslaved Africans" and decided to use it to more properly describe the New York Africans as people who had histories, experiences, and traditions that went far beyond slavery. Similarly, the descendant community asked that the use of the word "slaveowner" be avoided. Although the Euroamericans of that earlier period thought they "owned" enslaved Africans, in truth they held them captive against their will and forced them to work without pay. The descendant community argued that no one could "own" or control the emotions, minds, or identities of another human being. Descendants did not want the New York African Burial Ground project researchers or reports to use terms that uphold wrongs done in the past, and their requests were respected.

The team of experts gathered by Dr. Blakey and Howard University worked with the descendant community to identify four main topics of study for the project: origins, daily life, resistance to enslavement, and the development of African American identities. The researchers used advanced scientific methods to study these topics. Skeletal biologists studied human bones and teeth, DNA, isotopes, and population statistics.

History

History is the study of the past using written records, oral history, and physical objects. Historians learn about specific times and places by studying documents and by listening to what people remember about their past. For instance, historians can learn about a person's job and property ownership by studying a person's will, tax records, or census records. Marriage records, birth certificates, and death records can be used to learn when and where people lived and how they were related. Historians have to examine carefully how a document was made and where it came from to ensure the accuracy and meaning of the information it contains. Photographs, drawings, and maps can also be rich sources of information, as long as historians can determine when they were made, who made them, and what they depict. In some cases, historians can also talk to people living today to learn about their childhood or about the stories their parents or grandparents told them. For the New York African Burial Ground Project, little historical information was available for the actual people buried in the burial ground. At the same time, there was much information about the times and places in which they lived. This information allowed Director of the African Burial Ground History Component, Dr. Edna Greene Medford, and the project historians to develop a more detailed picture of the lives enslaved Africans had led in Africa, the Caribbean, and New York.

Archaeology

Archaeologists learn about the past by studying the objects people leave behind at a site and analyzing where those objects are found. To an archaeologist, context—the physical location of a find, including how it relates to other finds at a site—is everything. Much information can be gathered by examining where one find is located in relation to another. For example, at the New York African Burial Ground, archaeologists could determine that a grave pit found beneath another was placed earlier in time than the second grave pit. Therefore, the artifacts and human remains in the earlier grave pit would have been placed in the ground before the later grave pit was dug. The grave pit itself is a context, and the placement of artifacts within it—whether on the coffin lid, inside the coffin, or somewhere on the remains of the person buried there—can provide evidence related to burial practices, spiritual beliefs, or the identity of the individual in life.

At the New York African Burial Ground, the location of artifacts such as buttons, cuff links, and pins provided information about how those artifacts were used. Buttons found in a line along the outer thigh, for instance, could be interpreted as having been part of a pair of breeches. A metal ring on the finger could be interpreted as a finger ring, but if found in a cluster of rings at the neck, the ring could have been part of a necklace. Without context, archaeologists could not know whether these items were part of a garment, had been worn as a piece of jewelry, were held in a pocket or bundle, or had fallen accidentally into the grave fill. At the New York African Burial Ground, archaeologists led by Director for Archaeology Dr. Warren Perry used information from the context of the burials to learn when people were buried, how they were laid in the ground, how they were dressed, and which items were placed with them as offerings.

Example of a digital photographic series of an artifact (from Burial 366). This button was photographed from many angles to document its distinctive features (photographs by Jon Abbott).

Photograph of Burial 22, which contained a 2.5–4.5-year-old child, showing a fragment of hard-shell clam above the left clavicle. To the researchers, the shell's position indicated that the shell might have been strung and worn as a necklace (photograph by Dennis Seckler).

Clamshell fragment on the coffin lid of a 1–2-year-old child (Burial 348), near coffin's left shoulder break. Excavators found an iron nail beneath the shell. Researchers concluded the placement of the objects was probably deliberate (photograph by Dennis Seckler).

All images on this page are from The Archaeology of the New York African Burial Ground, *Part 1.*

Historians researched the background and lives of African New Yorkers from when they were free people in Africa, before they were enslaved, to their deaths in New York. Archaeological researchers examined how and where African-descended people were buried during the period of the burial ground's history and the artifacts placed in burials of that time. Together, all the results of these studies tell a rich and absorbing story of the lives of enslaved Africans in colonial New York. Readers of this book will find that the story of the New York Africans and their descendants is one of brutality and sorrow. It is also a story of dignity and triumph. It is an American story like no other.

Laboratory Director Mark Mack conducts dental recordation (from The Skeletal Biology of the New York African Burial Ground, *Part 1).*

Allison Davis and Keisha Hurst take anthropometric measurements (from The Skeletal Biology of the New York African Burial Ground, *Part 1).*

Archaeologists working under lights. Teams of two worked on each burial excavation, and the density of the grav es made for close quarters inside the shelters (photograph by Dennis Seckler) (from The Archaeology of the New York African Burial Ground, *Part 1*).

Excavation shelter erected at the New York African Burial Ground to allow archaeologists to work at the site at night and in the winter. The excavation shelter was illuminated by lights at night (photograph by Dennis Seckler) (from The Archaeology of the New York African Burial Ground, *Part 1*).

Slavery in New York

*B*efore the African Burial Ground was studied, few people other than historians knew that slavery was practiced in New York. Even today, many people think of slavery as something that happened only in the southern United States. Many people do not know that slavery was common in the northern states or in large cities like New York City. Slavery, which existed in New York City from the time it was first settled, was a central part of city life for more than 200 years.

The First European and African Settlers

The first European settlers in Manhattan were the Dutch. Before this, Manhattan had been home to a native people known as the Lenape, who had lived in the area for centuries. The Dutch arrived in 1624 and renamed the island New Amsterdam the following year. Eleven enslaved Africans were among the earliest settlers, arriving around 1626 according to many historians. Their names were Paulo Angola, Groot (Big) Manuel, Cleyn (Little) Manuel, Manuel de Gerrit de Reus, Simon Congo, Anthony Portugis, Gracia, Peter Santome, Jan Francisco, Cleyn Anthony, and Jan Fort Orange. Three enslaved women were brought shortly thereafter to work in Dutch homes. These few men and women founded the first African community in New Amsterdam.

New Amsterdam was small at first, with fewer than 300 residents in 1626. The population increased by approximately 100 new settlers in the first 10 years, and food and labor were in short supply. Grain, livestock, and vegetables had to be grown and tended. Houses, roads, a sawmill, a flour mill, and a fort needed to be built. New Amsterdam was under constant threat of Native American attacks, and so the Dutch West India Company (hereafter, the Company) forced enslaved Africans into military service to defend the settlement.

In New Amsterdam, Africans adjusted to a life of hard, thankless labor and few freedoms. They had more rights than enslaved people were later allowed, but they were still treated poorly. Under Dutch rule (1624–1664), enslaved

Settlement of New Amsterdam

The Dutch were the first Europeans to settle Manhattan Island. After Henry Hudson sailed up the Hudson River in 1609, Dutch merchants sent ships back to the river to trade with Native Americans for furs. Native Americans lived in two settlements on Manhattan but usually moved to other settlements during the winter. After a mutiny in 1613, the captains of three Dutch merchant ships and some of their crew became the first Europeans to spend the winter on Manhattan. A member of the crew, Jan Rodrigues, stayed on the island and became Manhattan's first settler of African descent. Rodrigues learned Native American languages and acted as a go-between for Native Americans and the Dutch.

The Dutch West India Company obtained exclusive rights to settle Manhattan in 1621. That same year, the Director-General of New Netherland "purchased" Manhattan Island from the local Native Americans, who believed the exchange was for temporary use rather than permanent ownership. Several years later, Manhattan was renamed New Amsterdam, and six farms were established along the shores of the island. The first settlers of New Amsterdam were Walloons, a Belgian minority who had escaped persecution in their homelands. Eleven enslaved Africans arrived the following year and were put to the task of building New Amsterdam.

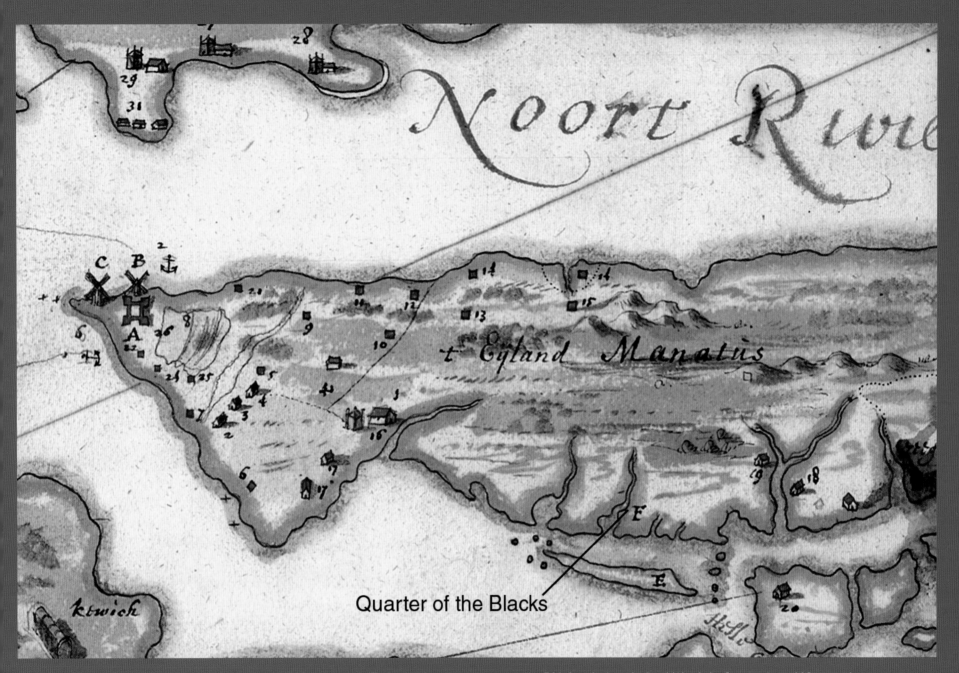

Quarter of the Blacks

Detail from the Manatus Map, depicting New Amsterdam in 1639, with a mark (F) showing the camp (near present-day 74th Street) where the Dutch West India Company housed African workers. The unnamed mapmaker provided the earliest known reference to slavery in New York on a map (Geography & Map Division, Library of Congress) (from The Archaeology of the New York African Burial Ground, Part 1).

Africans could own property, bring other colonists to court, marry Africans or non-Africans, and petition the authorities. Some learned to read and write, started families, and owned property on the outskirts of town. On the other hand, enslaved Africans had a lower status and did not own their labor. They were set apart in court records and could be bought and sold at auction.

Slavery and Commerce

New Amsterdam was first settled because of the fur trade. Native Americans and European trappers brought animal furs to trading posts like New Amsterdam, where furs were traded for other goods and shipped to Europe. There, they were used to make clothing, hats, and other items. In the early years, New Amsterdam exported as many as 15,000 animal pelts per year. Other exports soon followed, as farms were established in the region. Grain from area farms was milled in New Amsterdam and shipped to other port cities. As a port for seagoing ships, New Amsterdam traded with other colonies in the Americas and in Europe and Africa. Colonists exported manufactured goods, beer, liquor, and cloth. In return, they imported enslaved laborers and sugar, tobacco, cotton, and other items.

Enslaved Africans built and protected New Amsterdam. The Dutch West India Company recognized this and decided early on to import large numbers of enslaved Africans for their labor. Most of New Amsterdam's first Africans were captured during attacks on Portuguese ships carrying enslaved Africans from West Central Africa to the Caribbean. Later, enslaved Africans were brought into the colony on ships carrying trade items from the Caribbean. A ship that held hundreds of containers of goods might also have held several enslaved Africans as part of its cargo. Most enslaved Africans arrived in the colony this way, but the Company also shipped enslaved Africans directly from West Central Africa. In the mid-1600s, several shipments of 300 or more enslaved Africans landed at New Amsterdam; many were destined for re-export to other colonies. By 1660, about 350 Africans and their descendants, most of them enslaved, lived in New Amsterdam. Merchants in the city relied heavily on enslaved laborers, and business would have come to a grinding halt without them.

Land Grants and "Half Freedom"

After nearly 20 years of hard labor, some enslaved Africans in the colony received "half-freedom," which meant that they could own their own land and most of their labor. At the same time, they were forced to give a large amount of farm produce and a fat

Manuel de Gerrit de Reus

We will probably never know the names of most of the people buried at the African Burial Ground. African New Yorkers were given European names by their enslavers, but many also kept their original African names. Few records survive that list Africans by name or that chronicle the events of their lives, yet we know they worked, formed families, and were a part of the community. We do know some things about one African New Yorker, Manuel de Gerrit de Reus. New York African Burial Ground history researchers found de Reus's name in historical sources for several events spanning the decades of his life. These records revealed that he was one of the first 11 men brought to New Amsterdam as an enslaved laborer. In 1641, he was 1 of 8 men accused of killing a fellow African. Murder was a serious crime, and punishment was severe, but the authorities did not want to lose 8 valuable enslaved men so they chose one to pay for the crime: Manuel de Gerrit de Reus. However, when they tried to execute him by hanging, the rope broke. The crowd cried for the authorities to show him mercy, and he was pardoned. He later appears in the records as 1 of 6 Africans granted land in 1643 and also as 1 of 11 given conditional freedom in 1644.

NIEUW AMSTERDAM OFTE NUE NIEUW IORX OPT TEYLANT MAN

Gezicht op Nieuw Amsterdam by Johannes Vingboons (1664), an early picture of ships leaving and arriving at New Amsterdam. Ships like these would have brought enslaved Africans to the city's port.

hog to the Company each year. They also could be called upon at any time to work for the Company for a wage or for no money at all. For example, three women who were half-freed were made to clean houses on a weekly basis. People who broke the terms of their half-freedom were re-enslaved. Sadly, the children of people given half-freedom remained enslaved, and all children born after their parents were granted half-freedom were also to be enslaved.

Along with half-freedom, land grants on the northern edge of town were given to at least 28 Africans in 1644. These included the first 11 Africans enslaved by the Company. Many of these land grants were for property located close to the edge of the Collect Pond or along Broadway. The Company used half-freedom and landownership to set up a buffer of African homesites between the town and the local Native American settlements. When needed, Africans served as soldiers, and their homes were a first line of defense against attacks.

Most land grants were small, between 2 and 18 acres, but they were large enough to allow the African landowners to farm and raise animals. Eventually, a community of free and half-free Africans and Europeans grew on the edge of town. Timber houses with thatched roofs were surrounded by fields, where maize and other crops grew in summer. Cattle and hogs grazed on the stubble and on fallow ground. During winter, livestock were kept in barns and fed on hay prepared during the summer months.

Africans held on to their lands for as long as they could and willed them to their children. Some Africans bought more land. Solomon Pieters, for instance, purchased a 30-acre plot of land in 1680 near what became 23rd Street and Broadway. When he died in 1694, he left his house, land, and furniture to his wife and his tools and weapons to his sons. African landholdings became more valuable as the city grew, and African landowners increasingly were forced to sell their land and move to other areas. By the end of the 1600s, most African-owned land around the Collect Pond had been sold to people of European descent. Africans freed in New York City after 1712 were no longer allowed to own land.

The British Takeover

Life for the colony's enslaved Africans did not improve when the British took over New Amsterdam in 1664. The British changed the name of their new colony to New York in honor of James, Duke of York. James was the brother of the king of England,

A contemporary artist's depiction of New York Africans building a structure (illustration by Michael Colbert, 2004).

African Landholdings

By the 1660s, a large number of landowning black families lived near the African Burial Ground. Much of today's Washington Square Park was deeded to an African named Big Manuel. Paulo Angola's 6-acre grant extended between Minetta Lane and Thompson Street. Domingo Antony's 12-acre parcel stretched from near present-day Canal Street in the vicinity of Broadway to the Collect Pond, which was near present-day Franklin and Lafayette Streets. Simon Congo's 8-acre parcel centered on the intersection of present-day Varick and King Streets. Unfortunately, African landowners lost control of all of these lands as Euroamericans forced them to sell their land.

Detail from a map of Dutch-era land grants laid over a Manhattan street grid (ca. 1835) showing the approximate locations of patents issued to African men and women (the areas inside the heavy black lines) and Euroamericans Jan Jansen Damen and Cornelis Van Borsum. The map depicts the features of the seventeenth-century landscape—the pond, the swamps and wetlands, and the wagon roads. The African farms formed a loose arc around the northern side of Fresh Water Pond and the Cripplebush to the west; they were later sold to Europeans. (Source: Stokes [1915–1928 (6):Plates 84B-a and 84B-b]. On the creation of the map, see Stokes [1915–1928 (2):355–357].) (From The Archaeology of the New York African Burial Ground, Part 1.)

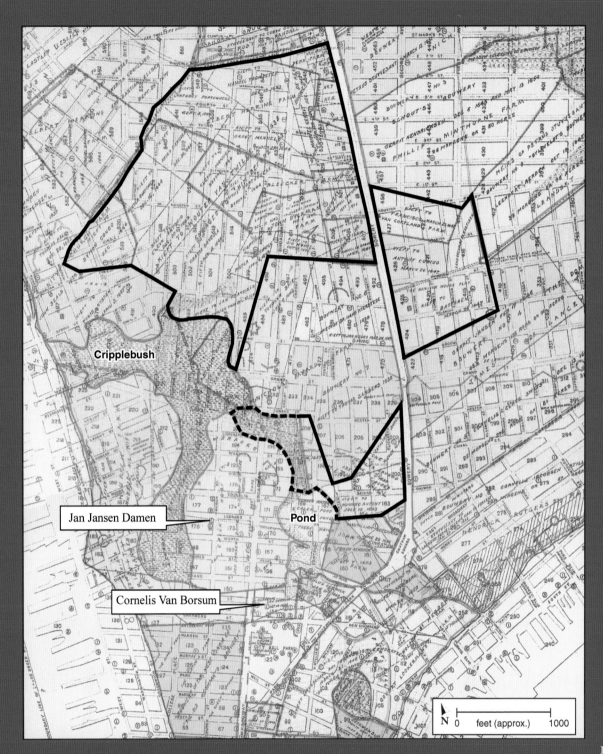

Charles II, who gave James control of New York and all colonies to the north. With James's rule came a strong British interest in slavery. James was a major shareholder in a company heavily involved in slavery: the Royal African Company.

The English were the largest importers of enslaved Africans to the Americas when the African Burial Ground was in use. Several years after the British takeover of New Amsterdam, the Dutch had left most of the West Central African and Caribbean trades to the British. Under the British, New York grew as a commercial center by exporting flour, biscuit, and other basic items to the Caribbean. Merchants in the city and farmers outside the city placed heavy demands on the enslaved Africans. In the early 1700s, 4 of 10 households depended on enslaved labor for cooking, cleaning, child care, craftwork, and serving guests. Some households rented out the labor of their enslaved Africans.

The British shipped most of the Africans they enslaved from West Africa to the Caribbean. The British also shipped enslaved Africans to North American colonies, like those of the Chesapeake and New York. The Royal African Company tried to sell enslaved Africans for fixed prices in Manhattan, but with little success. In the six decades after the British takeover, Royal African Company agents sold more than 2,000 enslaved Africans in Manhattan. Most of those enslaved by the British were shipped to New York City from the Caribbean as part of the provisions trade.

After Queen Anne's War (1702–1713), Britain acquired Spain's right to supply enslaved Africans to former Spanish colonies in the Caribbean and South America. New York's role in the Atlantic slave trade grew rapidly after that, and by 1720, the New York colony held more enslaved laborers than any other northern colony. New York was now importing five times as many enslaved Africans as in previous years. Those imports remained high for another 50 years.

Between 6,800 and 7,400 Africans arrived in the New York colony between 1700 and the eve of the Revolutionary War. A low estimate would be that about 2,800 people were imported directly from Africa and 4,000 from the Caribbean. Some also were brought in from the southern colonies. The true number is probably higher, because enslaved Africans were also smuggled into New York to avoid tariffs. Many enslaved people remained in New York City. Some gained legal freedom, but most died enslaved.

Until the 1740s, most Africans arrived in New York from the Caribbean, although there were occasional shipments of enslaved human beings direct from Africa. Thereafter, direct imports of enslaved laborers from West Africa became more important. These changing trade patterns played an important role in determining the age and sex makeup of the New York African population. The decline in Caribbean imports

A contemporary artist's depiction of New York Africans loading a ship (illustration by Michael Colbert, 2004) (from Historical Perspectives of the African Burial Ground).

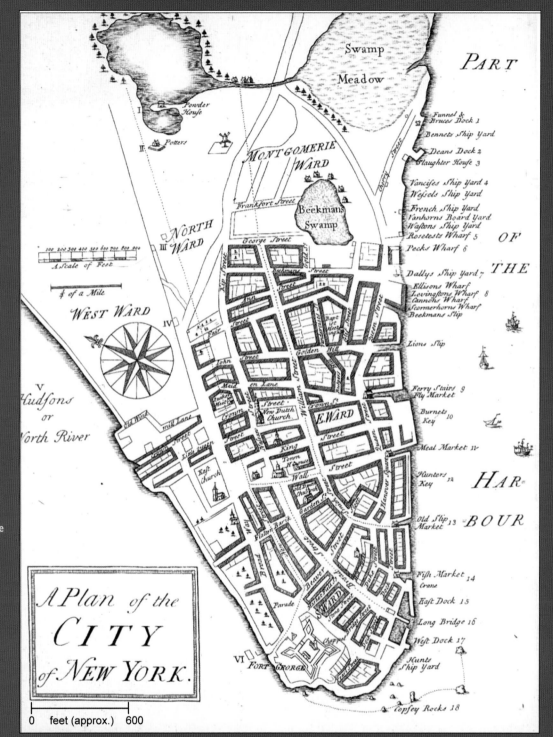

The Carwitham Plan, named for its engraver John Carwitham, was printed in London in 1740. By this time, New York was a bustling port city (Viscount Coke and the Trustees of the Holkham Estate) (from The Archaeology of the New York African Burial Ground, *Part 1).*

was probably a reaction to the alleged uprising of 1741 in New York or because Euroamerican authorities suspected that Africans who had spent time in the Caribbean were sometimes troublemakers and thus a potential threat to public safety.

The New York City economy shifted from one heavily concerned with agriculture and dock labor in the 1600s to a more urban marketplace in the 1700s. As a result, New York City's merchants shifted to importing more young people, especially girls, from Africa. By the mid-1700s, the demand for domestic servants purchased while young was constant. For example, in 1698 Jacobus Von Cortlandt wrote that the prime New York City market was for "Negroes between 15 and 20 years old." In December 1721, a New Yorker named Cadwallader Colden placed a newspaper ad to purchase a black girl about 13 years old to help with his children and sew. He also placed an ad for two young African men about 18 years of age, "strong and well-made for labor." Most enslavers in New York City held from one to three people captive, and many households had only a single domestic servant. This living arrangement differed from those in other areas where slavery was practiced, such as in the Caribbean and the Chesapeake colonies. In those areas, large groups of enslaved Africans lived in separate communities, apart from their captors, rather than in isolated households, as was the case in New York City.

Laws Against African Freedom

Shortly after the British takeover, the "Duke's Laws" were passed. Written to address nearly every aspect of life in the colony, some of these laws had the effect of restricting the rights of enslaved Africans and promoting the trade in enslaved Africans. Because these laws made it harder to employ indentured servants, colonists used enslaved Africans for labor instead. These laws also gave ships involved in slaving priority at warehouses and docks.

The British feared conspiracy and rebellion from the large number of enslaved Africans held in all parts of New York City. Consequently, in 1680, they passed many laws to stop enslaved Africans from gathering in groups larger than four people. They required Africans to obtain passes for traveling or to participate in group activities. Euroamerican residents were not allowed to do business with Africans or to provide entertainment to Africans in their homes. Africans were punished if they disturbed the peace, loitered in the streets on Sundays, or drank at bars. They also were no longer allowed to serve in the military.

Additional laws restricting African activities were passed in 1702. The 1702 laws restricted Africans' rights to do business, gather in groups, or move freely about the city.

Manumission

The act of freeing an enslaved laborer is called manumission. Some of the first enslaved Africans in New Amsterdam were given so-called "half-freedom" or limited rights after nearly two decades of slavery. Full freedom was very difficult for New York Africans to obtain and became even more so as Manhattan settlers became more reliant on enslaved labor. For example, Nero, an enslaved African held by the Dutch merchant Benjamin Faneuil, was half-freed in 1708. To be completely freed, however, he had to work for Faneuil and his family for another 10 years. In another case in 1691, a creditor claimed ownership of an African named Cresee after Cresee's enslaver died. Cresee was freed only after prominent citizens testified on his behalf that his enslaver had planned to free him. Few enslaved Africans had so much support. To free a person after 1712, enslavers had to pay a security that was five times higher than the going price of an enslaved adult. They also had to pay £20 per year for the upkeep of the person they freed. These fees made manumission costly and rare. Worse, manumission did not extend to the freed African's family. A freed person's children remained enslaved. Sometimes, free Africans paid money to free family members. In 1724, for example, the freedman John Fortune had saved enough to purchase the freedom of an enslaved woman, whom he married, and her son, who may have been his child. Still, the vast majority of enslaved Africans were never freed and died enslaved.

Advertisements for Enslaved Africans: The Specter of Sale

Enslaved Africans lived with the looming possibility that they could be sold and separated from family and loved ones at any time. Depending on the enslaver's financial situation and whim, even faithful and steady service to a seemingly appreciative enslaver was not enough to keep enslaved families together. This advertisement appeared in *The Daily Advertiser,* on June 8, 1793:

> To be sold: a black family, consisting of a man, his wife, a fine girl about twelve, another girl about five years old, and a male child capable of running about alone, the parents are honest, sober, neat, quiet, well disposed; have lived in the country; the man an excellent farmer, the woman a good cook, and excellent in a dairy; the eldest girl very handy in attending at table, the younger a child of hopes; in short, it is a useful trustworthy comely family, and of late years accustomed to live in this city. The above will be sold either separate or altogether.

Women might be sold simply because they were too fertile, as demonstrated by this advertisement that appeared in the May 27, 1751, edition of the *New York Gazette, revived in the Weekly Post Boy:*

> To be Sold, an excellent Negro Wench, about 20 years old, with a male child, about three months old; the Wench has had the Smallpox, can cook, wash, and iron, can be well recommended, and is Sold for no other Fault than being too fruitful.

Auction of an enslaved man during the Dutch Period (Harper's Monthly Magazine, 1895) *(from Historical Perspectives of the African Burial Ground).*

The laws also kept enslaved Africans from testifying against Euroamericans in court. A new public office—the "Whipper of slaves"—was created to handle punishment of law-breaking enslaved Africans. A few years after these so-called "slave codes" were passed, another even more restrictive law was passed. It stated that only people of African descent could be enslaved in New York and that the children of any enslaved African would also be enslaved. Further, conversion to Christianity could not be used as a reason to free the enslaved. As a result, it was nearly impossible for enslaved Africans in New York to become free after 1702.

Still more anti-African laws were passed after a revolt of enslaved laborers took place in 1712. Authorities at that time were afraid that the enslaved Africans and Euroamerican servants would join forces and rebel. The African community on the edge of the city was viewed as a place where enslaved and free Africans could easily plan escape or rebellion. After the 1712 Uprising, free Africans could no longer own real estate. The last piece of African-owned land in lower Manhattan was sold in 1716. The 1712 laws also made it very expensive to free an enslaved person. It cost around five times more money to free an enslaved African than to "buy" one, thus making it nearly impossible for an enslaver to grant freedom to an enslaved person.

British authorities also stepped up their efforts to control what Africans did under the cover of darkness. Enslaved laborers were forced to use a lantern so they could be seen while traveling at night. Dead Africans were to be buried only during the daytime. Cloths, or palls, could not be used to cover coffins so that weapons or other contraband could not be hidden underneath. Further, no more than 12 Africans could attend a burial of one of their own.

Any Euroamerican was allowed to whip an enslaved African who broke the law. Enslavers were fined heavily for crimes committed by enslaved Africans over whom they had control. The same laws were passed again in 1730, but with a twist. After 1730, enslaved Africans could only testify in court against other enslaved Africans and only for the crimes of arson, conspiracy, or murder.

Violence and Injury

Violence against enslaved Africans was pervasive. Enslavers beat and sometimes murdered enslaved Africans. Enslavers could be sentenced to death for murdering an enslaved African, however, and were fined £40 for mutilating one. Despite the law, enslavers were not always punished for violent crimes against enslaved Africans. In 1733, the Englishman William Petit beat Joe, an enslaved African, to death, but Petit

---

Restrictions on African Burials

The New York City Common Council passed a 1722 law restricting the burial of "all Negroes and Indian Slaves that shall dye within this corporation on the south side of the Fresh Water" to daylight hours. A 1731 amendment to the 1722 law reveals an intense fear of conspiracy:

> For the preventing of great numbers of slaves assembling and meeting together at their Funerals, under pretext whereof they have great opportunities of plotting and confederating together to do mischief, as well as neglecting their Masters Services it was ordered that, if more than twelve slaves assembled at a slave funeral, those present were to be whipped at the discretion of the Mayor, Recorder or one of the Alderman except the 12 slaves admitted by the owner of the dead slave, the gravedigger and the corpse bearers.

Punishments

When accused of a crime, Euroamericans in New York City were allowed a jury trial. Before 1788, enslaved or free Africans were not allowed a jury trial, only a tribunal of three justices of the peace and five prominent landowners was provided. Africans accused of theft were convicted twice as often as Euroamerican defendants using this system.

Punishments for breaking New York City's "slave codes" were brutal. In 1708, an enslaved African woman and an enslaved Native American man were executed for planning to murder the seven members of the Euroamerican Hallett family. Eighteen enslaved Africans were executed for participating in the 1712 Uprising, either by hanging or being burned at the stake. Another 30 Africans who were convicted in the 1741 conspiracy trials met similar fates. Even small offenses like theft were punished harshly. For stealing bags of coffee and candles, for example, an enslaved African named Cumbe was sentenced to 6 months of hard labor in the city jail. Other Africans were publicly whipped or even executed for similar offenses. For example, in 1719, an enslaved African named Harry was sentenced to death for theft. His old and feeble enslaver, Harmanus Burger, pleaded for mercy, claiming that he could not survive without Harry's labor. In 1719, an enslaved woman named Betty was convicted along with another woman for stealing a brass kettle. She was sentenced to be tied to a cart and whipped at various locations around the city, for a total of 39 lashes.

Execution of a New York African on the Common (from Valentine 1860) (from Historical Perspectives of the African Burial Ground).

was convicted of manslaughter rather than murder. Dutch farmer John Van Zandt whipped an enslaved African to death, but he was not prosecuted.

Broken bones represent evidence for violence or accidents. Twenty-three males and 18 females recovered from the New York African Burial Ground had fractured bones. Some of these fractures could have been caused by accidents. Others could have happened at the hands of enslavers. Among both the male and female remains, skull fractures were most common, most of them inflicted about the time of death. Men suffered numerous upper and lower limb fractures, but women suffered more broken hands and feet. Several individuals buried at the site had fractures throughout their body, suggesting either tragic accidents or extreme violence.

Researchers found that a woman aged between 15 and 24 (Burial 205) suffered the most fractures. She had broken bones throughout her body that occurred around the time of death. Her arms and legs were shattered, her backbone broken, and her skull fractured. A woman more than 50 years old (Burial 50) had two healed fractures of the right hand, and she suffered no less than eight breaks to her arms and legs, pelvis, and spine at time of death. One 45–55-year-old male (Burial 278) had more than 20 fractures. Only his skull escaped trauma. During his life, he had broken his collarbone but died either of injuries or a beating that broke his limbs, hip, and backbone. Another man aged 44–60 years (Burial 171) suffered four arm fractures during his lifetime and died from fractures to his skull, backbone, and rib cage.

Serious injuries extended to children as young as 11 years old. A 13–15-year-old boy (Burial 253) suffered from a fracture at the back of his skull and on the left temple during life. The left collarbone of another child aged 11–13 years (Burial 180) had been broken twice. His skull, limbs, and pelvis were broken around the time of death.

How did these injuries occur? Here the record is silent. Almost all the fractures identified on these individuals occurred at time of death. The potential for severe accidents during the lifetimes of those buried at the site was high, given the dangerous work environments of the era. Africans operated heavy carts, horses, boats, and mill equipment, all of which could crush a person to death. The skeletal biology researchers point out that enslaved Africans were also vulnerable to being beaten and murdered. In one instance, the evidence for violent death at the hands of an assailant—and possibly an enslaver—is clear. The researchers note that the 20–24-year-old woman in Burial 25 appeared to be resisting one or more persons with access to firearms when she died. A lead musket ball lodged in the woman's rib cage might have entered through her shattered left shoulder blade, leading the researchers to suggest that she might

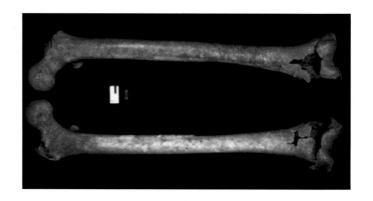

Fractures of the humerus (upper arm bone, above) and femora (thigh bones, below) in a female aged 18–20 years (Burial 205). Of all of the individuals recovered from the burial ground, this woman had the greatest number of fractures. All 32 fractures were perimortem (occurring near the time of death), suggesting she suffered from a severe accident or a violent death (from The Skeletal Biology of the New York African Burial Ground, Part 1*).*

Burial 25

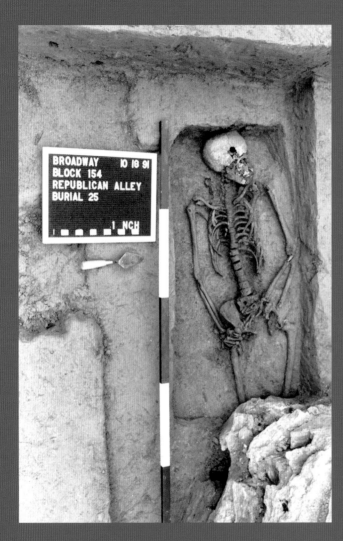

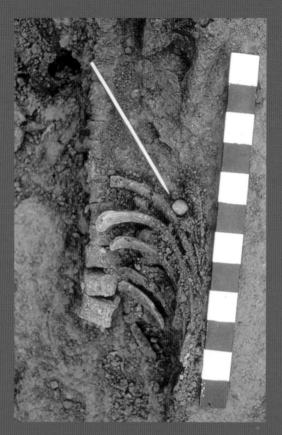

Musket ball lodged in rib cage of the woman in Burial 25 *(photograph by Dennis Seckler) (from* The Archaeology of the New York African Burial Ground, *Part 1).*

Photograph of Burial 25 during excavation. Bone fractures suggest that she suffered a blunt-force trauma to the face. The musketball lodged in her rib cage and her fractured lower arm are visible in the photographs to the right. Her burial was disturbed by the construction of a foundation wall for a building that once stood at 13 Duane Street *(photograph by Dennis Seckler) (from* The Archaeology of the New York African Burial Ground, *Part 1).*

Spiral fracture in lower arm of Burial 25 *(from* The Skeletal Biology of the New York African Burial Ground, *Part 1).*

have been shot in the back. She could have been taken by surprise or could have been running away from a pursuer. At some point, the woman had been grabbed by her lower right arm just above the wrist with a powerful twisting motion that broke her arm. She was also struck in the face, perhaps with a rifle butt. The researchers note that blows from a rifle butt would have been used to "finish off" a gunshot victim at that time. However, the researchers observed traces of new bone growth that suggest she lived a few days, probably in acute pain, before she died.

Dignity and Resistance

The enslaved Africans of New York did not stand idly by in the face of all these wrongs. They fought the system of slavery and fought as well to hold on to their dignity. They passed on to their children African beliefs and traditions and celebrated their diverse African heritages. Gathering in the streets, taverns, and in the countryside, they shared songs, dance, and stories, often in secret. They formed families and had children. Early on, some owned land and controlled their own labor. And at the African Burial Ground, they buried loved ones in African-controlled spaces following their unique African traditions.

Enslaved Africans also used many strategies to subvert their enslavers and resist the theft of their labor. Although the enslavers stole this labor and provided little to the Africans in return, whenever possible the enslaved Africans secretly hired themselves out for pay. Sometimes they performed skilled jobs so well that Euroamericans lost jobs as a result. To provide food and clothes for their families, Africans also stole from their enslavers. A huge underground market, in which many Euroamericans also participated, evolved so that enslaved Africans could buy and sell goods they were not legally allowed to exchange. To resist forced labor, enslaved Africans broke tools, talked back, dragged their feet, and faked illness. Some slipped away from their enslavers for days at a time, often to see loved ones, and those who knew how to read and write forged passes for traveling. And whenever they could, enslaved Africans escaped.

Some Africans also lashed out with violence against their enslavers. They burned down the Euroamericans' houses and taverns. They poisoned them. They attacked Euroamericans to escape or to protect loved ones. The examples of such resistance that we know about are in the historical record because many of those Africans who rebelled violently were caught. In the 1690s, an enslaved African named Prince assaulted the mayor of New York, William Merritt, in the face when the mayor tried to break up a group of Africans for disturbing the peace near his home. Prince was publicly whipped

Rebellion

Enslaved Africans openly rebelled throughout the colonial Americas. An uprising occurred in New York City in 1712, and an alleged conspiracy to rebel was rumored in 1741. In 1526, enslaved Africans held by the Spanish in what, under British control, later became South Carolina rebelled and escaped within a few months of their arrival. Enslaved Africans revolted in Mexico multiple times in the 1500s and 1600s. In Jamaica, revolts were common from the 1670s to the 1730s. In the North American colonies, revolts occurred in 1739 in Stono, South Carolina, and in 1743, in Newport, Rhode Island. In the 1790s, enslaved Africans revolted in Haiti. In 1811, Charles Deslondes, a free Haitian of African descent, led a rebellion of several hundred enslaved Africans in Louisiana. Other revolts were planned but never carried out. Enslaved Coromantee planned revolts in St. Croix in 1759 and in Jamaica in 1760. In 1801, armed forces stopped Gabriel's plan to organize more than a thousand enslaved Africans to attack Richmond's Euroamerican population.

Rebellions also took place on slaving vessels during the trip from Africa to the Americas, called Middle Passage. Senegambians, who were common in New York, were particularly rebellious during the transport stage. Rebellions of captured and enslaved Africans were reported in newspapers like the *New-York Weekly Post-Boy* and were an increasing source of alarm for New York enslavers and other residents during the 1700s.

Grave Markers

Cemeteries are as much for the living as for the dead, and grave markers allow mourners and relatives to return to the graves of their loved ones for years after the funeral. Visits to lay flowers or carry out additional rituals are commonplace. During the time the African Burial Ground was in use, enslaved Africans probably held one or more ceremonies at graves months or years after burial, just as they had done in Africa. In some African societies, small structures were built over graves, where ceremonies were held and offerings placed. The practice of leaving offerings persisted in North America. African American graves in the 1800s were marked with bottles and jars. These artifacts often were broken through the base, so they could no longer be used by the living.

Most likely then, the African Burial Ground would have been a sea of grave markers. Wooden posts, rectangular stone slabs, or rows of cobbles were all used to mark graves. Some graves had rectangular stone slabs placed vertically near the head of the grave, like those of a 35–45-year-old, probably a woman (Burial 18), and a 25–35-year-old man (Burial 23). Rows of small stone cobbles delineated some interments. The grave of a 2–4-year-old child (Burial 13/43) was outlined with a double arc of cobbles. These cobble grave markers likely were tended until the area was covered over with fill. The grave of a 35–45-year-old man (Burial 47) was marked with an upright stone slab and possibly a row of cobbles along the north side of the grave. The upright stone was placed near the head of the person in Burial 47 but may have also been used to mark the location of other nearby burials. Other graves were marked with wooden posts or with boards connected to the head or foot of coffins. A man between 30 and 40 years old (Burial 194) lay in a coffin with a wooden board used to mark the grave above ground.

Excavated grave of Burial 18 with stone marker in place at its west (head) end. Arrows point to the coffin outlines of Burial 7, cutting into the north profile, and Burial 11, at the lower left. Both of these graves lay above the coffin in Burial 18   (photograph by Dennis Seckler).

Stone that appears to have been a marker for Burial 23 (photograph by Dennis Seckler).

Stone marker for Burial 23 in relation to nearby lines of cobbles   (photograph by Dennis Seckler).

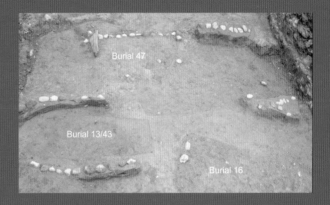

Burials at the southwest corner of the excavated cemetery that were marked with cobbles at the surface. This style of grave marking has been observed throughout the African Diaspora over a broad span of time   (photograph by Dennis Seckler).

Vertical slab of stone found above Burial 47 and the line of cobbles along the north side of the grave (photograph by Dennis Seckler).

All images on this page are from The Archaeology of the New York African Burial Ground, *Part 1.*

at every major intersection in town. Many other Africans were punished or executed for assault, murder, or the attempted murder of their enslavers and other whites.

One major example of such known violent resistance was the 1712 Uprising. On April 1, 1712, more than two dozen Africans set fire to a New York City building owned by the Euroamerican baker Peter Vantilborough, who held other enslaved Africans captive. The rebels ambushed the settlers who came to put out the fire. Using guns, hatchets, knives, and other stolen weapons, the rebels killed 8 Euroamericans and injured 12. No rebels were killed during the attack. Several escaped to the countryside; others committed suicide rather than be captured. Seventy suspected rebels were jailed, and 21 were tried and convicted. Akan-speaking Coromantee and Pawpaw laborers who had recently arrived in New York were among those captured. Two "Spanish Negroes," Hosey and Juan, were also accused of revolt. They, however, had insisted since their arrival that they were free Spanish subjects. Eighteen of the convicted rebels were executed. Some were burned at the stake, and others were hanged. All were beheaded and their bodies left to rot in the streets. Peter the Doctor, a free African conjurer who may have led the rebellion, was kept in jail for months but eventually set free.

Another major event happened in 1741, the day after a disorderly St. Patrick's Day celebration. That time, most of the buildings inside the city's fort were burned to the ground. Nine other fires took place over several weeks thereafter. New Yorkers feared the fires were part of a huge conspiracy and worried that large numbers of Africans and their Euroamerican allies planned to burn down the city and escape by boat. Enslavers feared they would be murdered and their women raped. Authorities arrested 160 Africans and 21 Euroamericans. Four Euroamericans were hanged, and 30 Africans were hanged or burned at the stake. The executions of the accused African conspirators took place in the Common near the burial ground.

Today, most scholars agree that no big conspiracy had been planned in 1741. The trials revealed, however, that enslaved Africans talked regularly about theft, murder, and destruction of their enslavers' property. Sometimes, they did more than talk: they joined together or struggled alone to take what was denied them and defy the restrictive laws that prevented them from enjoying freedom and opportunity.

Escape

A few enslaved Africans escaped to distant communities in British New York where a mix of Native Americans, Euroamericans, and African Americans had started a new life free of slavery and indentured servitude. These settlements, called Maroon communities,

Maroon Communities

Africans who escaped slavery in the Americas often formed Maroon communities, which were particularly common in the Caribbean and in South America. Maroons hunted and fished for their own food and raided nearby Euroamerican communities, oftentimes living with Native Americans or Euroamericans trying to escape criminal prosecution. In the New York region, Maroon communities do not appear to have formed because of the geography of Manhattan Island and the presence of large numbers of armed Euroamericans in New York City.

Small groups of escapees were reported in rural areas outside the city, however. In 1679, enslaved Africans began escaping to eastern Long Island to live among Native American communities. In 1690, farmers in Harlem complained of escapees raiding their village. In the same year, the French explorer Sieur de Villiers came across a community of Native Americans, Europeans, and escaped Africans while traveling between Lake Ontario and the Canisteo River Valley. During and after the Revolutionary War, thousands of escapees fled to New York City to hide. Escapees were often pursued by posses seeking a reward for their capture.

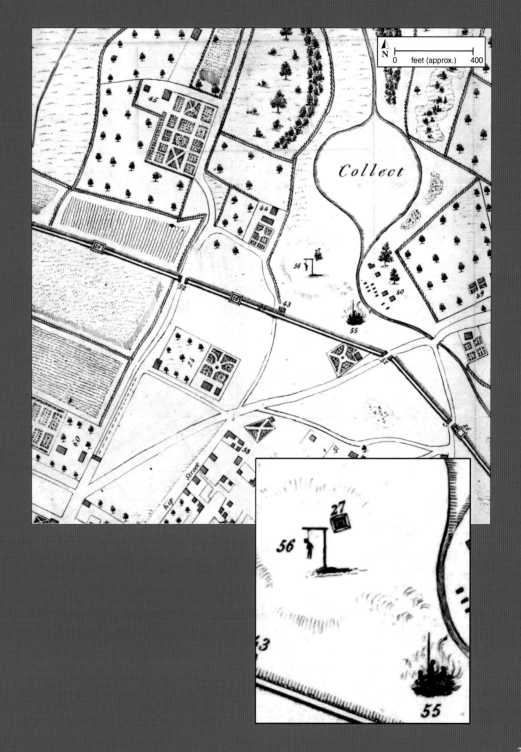

Detail from New Yorker David Grim's recollection of the city in 1742–1744, showing two of the punishments inflicted on Africans convicted of conspiring to set fire to the town. The stake at which some of the conspirators were burned (No. 55) is set across from a tannery (No. 40). A box representing the powder house (No. 27) is near the scaffold where Africans were hung (No. 56). Northwest of the scaffold are the Remmey & Crolius Pottery (No. 44) and the neatly laid gardens of the Rutgers estate (No. 45) (The Lionel Pincus and Princess Firyal Map Division, The New York Public Library, Astor, Lenox and Tilden Foundations) (from The Archaeology of the New York African Burial Ground, Part 1).

were common throughout the Americas. Some of the largest were in South America, where most of the Africans enslaved during the transatlantic slave trade were sent. Small settlements of African escapees also existed outside Manhattan. In the late 1600s, for example, gangs of escapees were noted in outlying areas of the city such as Harlem and eastern Long Island. Gangs of escapees were also written about in the 1740s. One was noted near Lake Ontario, and larger settlements were identified farther away.

Most of the African escapees were American-born adult males. This was because the jobs assigned to men typically allowed them to move around outside more and over larger areas. Women and children were often confined to homes and individual properties. It was also more accepted for a man, even an enslaved African man, to be out and about during the colonial era. Because enslaved people born in America had more knowledge of the local language and customs than those born in Africa or newly arrived in America, they could escape more easily. They were more likely to fool passersby into thinking they were either free or allowed to travel. The greatest number of escapes happened during the Revolutionary War (1775–1783) and in the late 1790s and early 1800s. During the Revolutionary War, the British army took control of New York City. At the beginning of the war, the British offered freedom to all enslaved laborers and indentured servants who enlisted in British military service. They also gave enslaved Africans paid work as blacksmiths, builders, carpenters, river pilots, soldiers, and wagon drivers. As a result of British war policy, thousands of escapees fled from other colonies to New York City. The city itself became a kind of Maroon community. In that environment, enslaved women and children were able to escape as well as men. When the war ended, the British helped more than 3,000 free Africans move to places like Nova Scotia, New Brunswick, England, and Sierra Leone. However, life remained hard for the escapees, who then had to struggle with new environments, few supplies, and persistent racism in their new communities.

The Legal End of Slavery

In New York, legal steps to end the trade in enslaved Africans began in the mid-1780s, after the Revolutionary War had ended. The New York State legislature tried to end slavery in 1785, but its bill was rejected by the Council of Revision. The legislature did, however, end the need to pay a large fee to free an enslaved African. This made it easier for enslavers to free the enslaved. Three years later, "buying" or "selling" enslaved Africans for export was made illegal in New York State. The state also made enslavers teach enslaved laborers born after 1788 to read and gave enslaved Africans the right to trial by jury.

Ways to Escape

Enslaved Africans traveled around New York City regularly. Many also worked as sailors in the shipping industry. Several took advantage of their mobility to escape. Escape was fairly common for African sailors who worked on privateering vessels. Privateers were private war ships that attacked ships of other nations to obtain their cargo. By 1702, city authorities feared that many enslaved Africans were fleeing New York City by boat. In the 1740s, intense privateering led to many escapes.

Capturing escapees depended on the townspeople's help. Advertisements describing an escapee's appearance, language use, skills, and clothing were used to alert citizens of escapes. To escape, enslaved Africans had to fool passersby into thinking they were not trying to run away. Those who knew how to write forged passes for travel and faked manumission or free birth. When necessary, they also took violent action. In 1749, four enslaved Africans from New Spain murdered the crew of a sailboat in New York's port, hijacked the vessel, and escaped by sea.

During the Revolutionary War, 80,000–100,000 enslaved Africans escaped bondage in all of British North America. Around 12,000 escaped to New York City. Thousands left the city again after the War, but about 4,000 escapees stayed. In the late 1700s and early 1800s, thousands of escapees, free Africans, and indentured Africans lived in New York City. With so many Africans in the city, it was possible for Africans to hide within the city itself or to escape to the countryside. During this time, escape was many times more common in New York than in the southern states.

Burial 259

For enslaved African women, masking one's identity as a man could have served many purposes, including helping one to escape. Historical accounts note that some female enslaved Africans were suspected by enslavers of trying to pass for men. At the New York African Burial Ground, there was one instance of a 17–19-year-old identified as a probable woman buried in men's clothing (Burial 259). The placement of 18 buttons and textile fragments around her legs and pelvic area suggests she wore breeches and a shirt when she was laid to rest. Four buttons of identical ridged-face design were lined up along her upper leg, just above the knee, and three similar buttons were present in the pelvic area. The researchers concluded that the buttons were clearly from breeches. Woven wool textile fragments were associated with buttons on the pelvic area and the knees, and one had a well-preserved buttonhole. Two buttons, possibly with leather covers, from the ribs of the probable woman indicate she wore a shirt along with the knee breeches. Because researchers were not able to positively identify the sex of this individual, it is possible that Burial 259 held a slender young man wearing knee breeches. Yet there are several reasons a woman might be wearing men's clothing in colonial New York, among them, greater freedom of movement within the community and the possibility of working in trades typically reserved for men, such as privateering. It is also possible that the woman was a recent escapee trying to disguise her identity by appearing to be an individual of the opposite sex.

All images on this page are from The Archaeology of the New York African Burial Ground, *Part 1.*

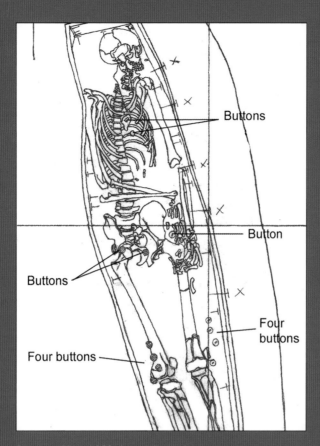

Drawing of Burial 259 showing button locations (drawing by M. Schur).

Copper-alloy buttons, with parallel ridged and milled decoration, from Burial 259 (photograph by Jon Abbott).

Tin-plated, copper-alloy button from Burial 259 (photograph by Jon Abbott).

Textile from Burial 259, retrieved from coffin wood sample (photograph by Jon Abbott).

Button with associated cloth (left) and removed to show the buttonhole (right). The cloth did not appear to have been top stitched (photograph by Jon Abbott).

Possible leather-covered wood buttons from Burial 259 (photograph by Jon Abbott).

The new federal government did little to improve the rights of enslaved Africans. Congress even passed the Fugitive Slave Act of 1793, which allowed bounty hunters to pursue escaped Africans into northern states. The act also allowed citizens to help catch escapees. However, groups such as the New York Manumission Society protected many African escapees and people accused of helping Africans escape slavery.

A law to end slavery was finally passed in New York State in 1799, but it did not do away with slavery immediately. New York legislators feared that a sudden end to slavery would cause the state's economy to fall apart. Instead, they ruled that the children of the enslaved were to be considered freed only after years of work as indentured servants. The male children of enslaved mothers were indentured to their mother's enslavers for 28 years, and female children, for 25 years. Under the new law, enslavers were also to be compensated for raising the children of enslaved Africans, and they were permitted to abandon African newborns to the state after 1 year of care.

The federal government banned the importation of enslaved Africans to America in 1808. That same year, the New York State legislature passed an act to prevent the kidnapping of people of African descent for the purpose of enslaving them, but illegal kidnapping continued nonetheless. Many victims of this crime were sent to Cuba or South America to be enslaved.

Enslaved Africans living in New York were legally emancipated on July 4, 1827. No major official celebrations were held for fear of riots. African American New Yorkers celebrated their Emancipation Day with quiet, private celebrations on July 4, but more than 2,000 African Americans marched peacefully from John's Park to Zion Church on July 5 to mark the occasion. Slavery was evident in New York for more than a decade afterward, however. By law, nonresidents were allowed to enter the state with their enslaved laborers until 1841, and they continued to do so illegally into the 1860s. Slavery was ended throughout the United States after the close of the Civil War in 1865 with the ratification of the 13th Amendment to the Constitution of the United States. Though slavery was no longer legally allowed in the United States, the impacts of slavery and racism, its accompanying evil, are still felt to this day.

Societies

In the 1740s, a religious movement called the Great Awakening took the stand that slavery is immoral. The movement considered Africans and Europeans the same in moral terms, breaking from previous perceptions that Africans were immoral. Quakers in New York and Philadelphia began asking enslavers to leave their congregations in the 1770s. Still, New York City Quakers were among the last to rid their lives of slavery and did not invite Africans into their congregations. The New York Manumission Society was formed in 1785 by elite Euroamerican Quakers and members of the Church of England. Founders included John Jay, future Chief Justice of the United States, and Alexander Hamilton, future United States Secretary of the Treasury. The society provided legal aid to Africans and protected escapees but favored only gradual emancipation. In 1787, it established the African Free School, a single-room school for boys and girls at 245 William Street.

Africans also formed their own societies to promote the education and welfare of African New Yorkers. The New York African Society, a benevolent and spiritual organization, was formed in 1784. It was short-lived but served as the basis for later societies, like the New York African Society for Mutual Relief founded in 1808. Other societies included the Brooklyn African Woolman Benevolent Society and Zion Church's African Marine Fund, both established in 1810. These societies took active and public roles in helping the African American community. Individuals also spearheaded efforts to promote the education of Africans in New York. Catherine Ferguson, an African American cake maker, established an integrated Sunday school in 1793 for children of African or European descent. Schools and societies helped Africans achieve success on their own terms in America and combat racism in other social institutions.

Family

Although we have no direct evidence, we can be sure that the individuals buried at the African Burial Ground shared bonds based on family, love, friendship, and community. Africans in colonial New York had extended family ties and formed bonds with nonrelatives. Sadly, the sale of enslaved Africans separated families, taking husbands from wives and children from their parents. To strengthen family ties, Africans reclaimed orphans, widows, and widowers through adoption and marriage. Enslaved Africans also witnessed each other's marriages and served as godparents when children were baptized. These practices served to renew and strengthen family ties among Africans. For example, when Catalina Van Angola died, her widower Anthony Van Angola married Lucie, the widow of Laurens d'Angola. Their wedding, on May 5, 1641, was among the first of several marriages between Africans recorded in New Amsterdam's Dutch Reformed Church. Their son Anthony was christened in August 1643, and Dorothy D'Angola, widow of Paolo d'Angola, stood as godmother. She and her second husband adopted the child when he became orphaned as an infant. They petitioned for his freedom in 1661, when he turned eighteen, and it was granted.

Other possible family ties are suggested by the findings of New York African Burial Ground Project researchers. In one instance of a possible shared grave, the 40–50-year-old man in Burial 314 and the 33–65-year-old woman in Burial 338 were buried in hexagonal coffins placed side by side. Their advanced ages and the closeness of their burials could suggest a commitment and connection in life based in family ties, friendship, or love that endured in the face of adversity. We can never know the exact ties that existed between these individuals, but we can be sure that family and community groupings are represented at the burial ground.

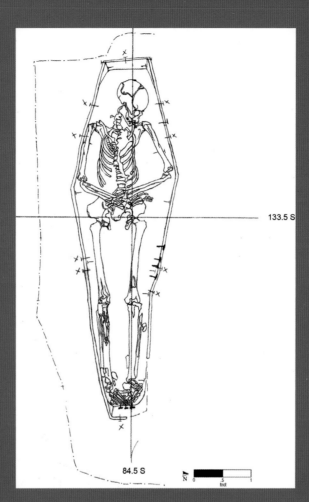
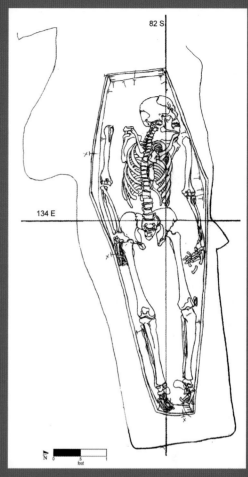

Burial 338 (left), which held a 33-65-year-old woman, was buried side by side with Burial 314 (right), which held a 40-50-year-old man. These individuals might have shared a grave (drawings by M. Shur) (from The Archaeology of the New York African Burial Ground, Part 2).

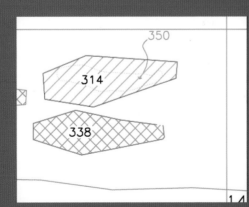

Inset from the project site plan showing Burials 314 and 338 side by side (from The Archaeology of the New York African Burial Ground, Part 1).

The African Burial Ground Through Time

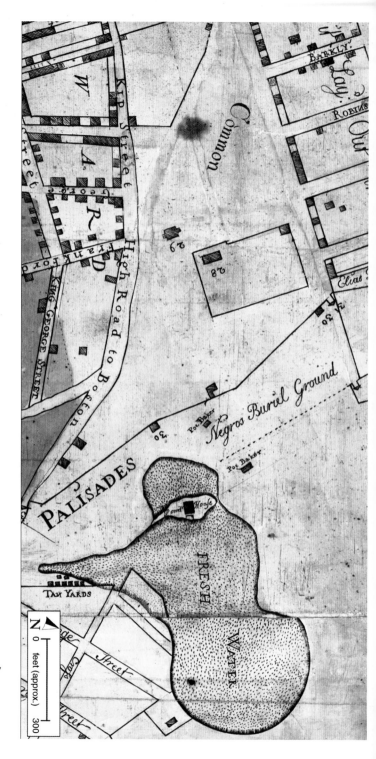

The African Burial Ground may have first been used around 1650, when African families were living north of the city near the Collect Pond. The

Chapter 3 excavated portion of the African Burial Ground at 290 Broadway in Block 154 (bounded by Broadway, Duane, Reade, and Elk Streets) is only a small portion of the 6-acre burial ground. The 0.22-acre area where burials were excavated represents less than 4 percent of the original burial ground. The rest remains under buildings and pavements in New York City. Some of the burial ground was certainly destroyed over many years, but other parts could still be intact below ground.

Much of the burial ground was located on an area long ago known as the Common. In the 1600s, many European settlements had an area that the public could use for things like grazing cattle or cutting timber. In New York City, the Common was located on the north edge of the city next to the Collect Pond, where fresh water was available. During Dutch rule, the Common was mostly open space. During British rule, the Common was taken over by the city. Industries that needed fresh water or produced toxic fumes, such as beer breweries, tanneries, and slaughterhouses, were located on the Common. The 1754 Maerschalk Plan shows the Common and the tanneries (labeled "Tan Yards") and potteries (labeled "Pot Baker") near the Fresh Water Pond.

Detail from the Maerschalk Plan, 1754. The "Negros Buriel Ground" is clearly labeled between Fresh Water Pond and the Common. The dashed diagonal line corresponds to the approximate northern boundary of the Van Borsum patent and probably also of the African Burial Ground. Also shown is a palisade wall that crossed the southern portion of the Van Borsum Patent. The "Common" is today's City Hall Park, with Broadway running along its west side. The Almshouse (No. 28) and a powder house (No. 29) stood on the Common (Geography & Map Division, Library of Congress) (from The Archaeology of the New York African Burial Ground, Part 1*).*

Sample Size

Archaeologists refer to the burials from one site or portion of a site as a sample. A sample is only a portion of what the entire site represents. For instance, if there were 100 burials and only 10 were excavated, the 10 burials in the sample represent 10 percent of 100 burials. Depending on how it is selected, a sample may or may not accurately represent the total from which it is taken. The excavated area was only a small portion of the original 6-acre burial ground. As a result, only a small number of the thousands of burials in the African Burial Ground were excavated, and the burials that were excavated may not be similar to burials in other parts of the burial ground.

Sanborn Map of New York's civic center area, encompassing the historic African Burial Ground at the time of the initial investigation in 1989. The small portion of the cemetery that was excavated in 1991–1992 is outlined with a red line within the boundary of the African Burial Ground National Historic Landmark (outlined with a thick black line). Most of Block 154, bounded by Broadway and Duane, Reade, and Elk Streets, was covered by parking lots. The map shows the historic "Calk Hook Farm" (labeled in upper left corner) and its southern boundary running diagonally from Broadway across the block. The historic edge of the Collect Pond is shown at the upper right (use of 1984-85 Sanborn Map 290 Broadway, New York, NY, reprinted/used with permission from the Sanborn Library, LLC) (from The Archaeology of the New York African Burial Ground, *Part 1).*

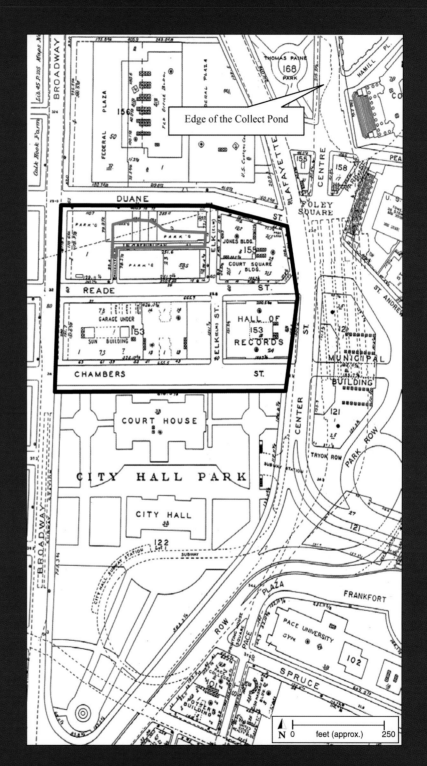

Edge of the Collect Pond

The Common was also used for prisons and human burials. During the 1700s, the city built a powder house, an almshouse for the poor, palisades, barracks, and a city prison on the Common. Public gatherings also were held on the Common. These included executions of Africans in 1741, when enslaved Africans and Europeans were accused of plotting to overthrow the city. Executions took place on the Common, probably near the African Burial Ground. On the eve of the Revolutionary War, the city ordered all free and enslaved Africans to build fortifications on the Common. Enslaved Africans worked every day, and free Africans every other day, to build those fortifications. Revolutionary War deserters and prisoners of war were buried behind the barracks on the Common, and some probably were placed in the African Burial Ground. Some of these burials could have been placed between Reade Street and Chambers Street, which is outside of the excavated portion of the New York African Burial Ground at 290 Broadway.

City Lots

The excavated area was in the northern area of the larger African Burial Ground. During its use, this part of the burial ground lay within two city lots: Calk Hook Farm Lot No. 2 and the Van Borsum patent. These lots changed hands several times while the burial ground was in use. Lots were divided up, and houses were built on these lots. Calk Hook Farm Lot No. 2 contained a small portion of the site near the northern edge of the burial ground. Most of the site was within the Van Borsum patent. The limits of the Van Borsum patent today are roughly between Broadway, Duane Street, Centre Street, and Chambers Street. Descriptions of these lots made in 1673 and 1696 do not mention the burial ground. Perhaps the area was not heavily used for burial at the time, or the burial ground was not considered worth mentioning.

During excavation, archaeologists found many broken pieces of pottery and pieces of animal bone in grave features. These artifacts appeared to be trash from a nearby pottery and a tannery, which processed animal hides to make leather. A stoneware pottery built around 1730 near the southeast corner of the Van Borsum patent and another located north of the burial ground probably dumped trash on the burial ground. When graves were dug, trash from the pottery and tannery littered the ground surface and made its way into fill dirt.

In the 1760s, Isaac Teller built houses and lots along Broadway within the burial ground, and construction on these lots probably disturbed previous burials.

The Van Borsum Patent, issued in October 1673 under Governor Colve's signature, describes the boundaries of an outlying parcel that came to be known as the African Burial Ground. The patent was damaged in a fire at the New York State Library, Albany, in 1911 (New York State Archives; Series A1881-78, Dutch Colonial Administrative Records, 1673–1674, Vol. 23, 20–433) (from The Archaeology of the New York African Burial Ground, Part 1).

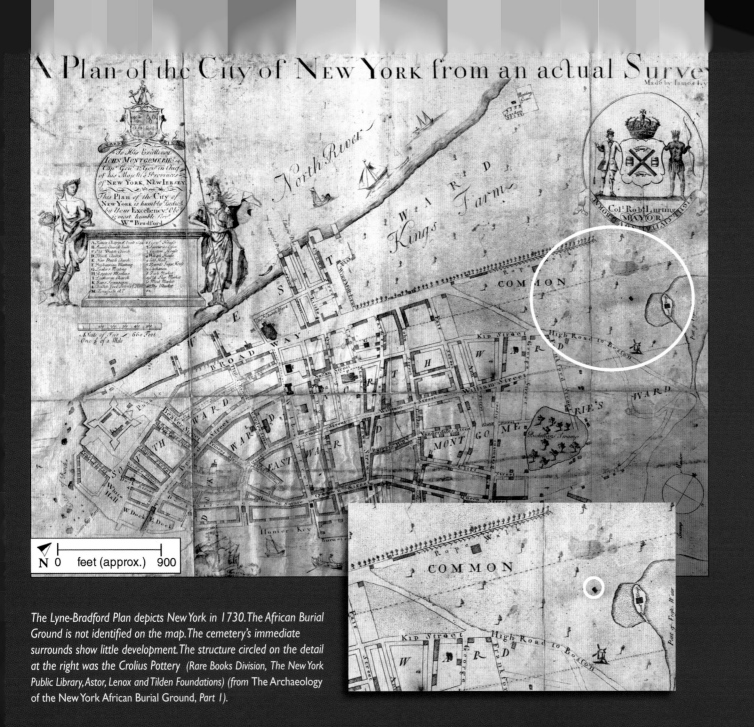

Sherds, or broken pieces of pottery, from the grave shafts of Burial 353 (top) and Burial 333 (bottom). The broken pottery was probably deposited as trash from potteries near the burial ground, possibly the Crolius Pottery circled in the inset map to the left (from The Archaeology of the New York African Burial Ground, *Part 3).*

The Lyne-Bradford Plan depicts New York in 1730. The African Burial Ground is not identified on the map. The cemetery's immediate surrounds show little development. The structure circled on the detail at the right was the Crolius Pottery (Rare Books Division, The New York Public Library, Astor, Lenox and Tilden Foundations) (from The Archaeology of the New York African Burial Ground, *Part 1).*

By this time, construction around all four sides of the African Burial Ground left less area for burials. In 1768, Teller apparently built a fence around a portion of the burial ground and charged fees for entry. Teller's houses and the fence were taken down by the British during the Revolutionary War (1775–1783).

Places of Burial

In the 1600s, a large number of landowning African families lived near the African Burial Ground. Many of the land parcels granted to Africans by the Dutch were located on the north and west edges of the Collect Pond. Peter Stuyvesant, Governor of New Amsterdam, relocated some African farmers to farms near his along Broadway in 1659 and 1660. By the 1680s, a community of Africans, Europeans, and people of mixed descent were living along Broadway north of the city.

During the 1600s, many Africans in Manhattan would have been buried in farm plots, church yards, town cemeteries, or the African Burial Ground. The African Burial Ground could have been in use as early as 1650, when Africans lived nearby. The sloping land near the Collect Pond was not the best for residences or farming. Because they had no use for it, landowners may have allowed it to be used for burial. The African Burial Ground was almost certainly in use by 1697. In that year, the Anglican Trinity Church forbade burials of Africans in its cemetery:

> Ordered, That after the Expiration of four weeks from the dates hereof no Negroes be buried within the bounds & Limits of the Church Yard of Trinity Church, that is to say, in the rear of the present burying place & that no person or Negro whatsoever, do presume after the terme above Limited to break up any ground for the burying of his Negro, as they will answer it at their perill

This order could have led to heavier use of the African Burial Ground, with Africans having few other options for burial. The first known record of the African Burial Ground dates to 1712. In that year, Chaplain John Sharpe wrote that Africans were "buried by those of their own country and complexion in the common field, without any Christian office; perhaps some ridiculous Heathenish rites were performed at the grave by some of their own people." A map of the city showing the burial ground was not drawn until Mrs. Buchnerd produced her hand-drawn plan in the 1730s.

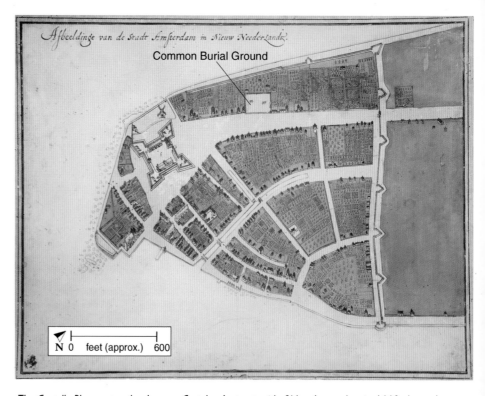

The Castello Plan, mapmaker Jacques Cortelyou's street grid of New Amsterdam in 1660, shows the common burial ground on the west side of the wagon road (Broadway), midway between the fort and the wall (Wall Street) (I. N. Phelps Stokes Collection, Miriam and Ira D. Wallach Division of Art, Prints and Photographs, The New York Public Library, Astor, Lenox and Tilden Foundations) (from The Archaeology of the New York African Burial Ground, *Part 1).*

View of Trinity Churchyard, October 2005. The Anglican Trinity Church forbade burials of Africans in its cemetery in 1697, probably leading to more intensive use of the African Burial Ground (photograph by Rob Tucher) (from The Archaeology of the New York African Burial Ground, *Part 1).*

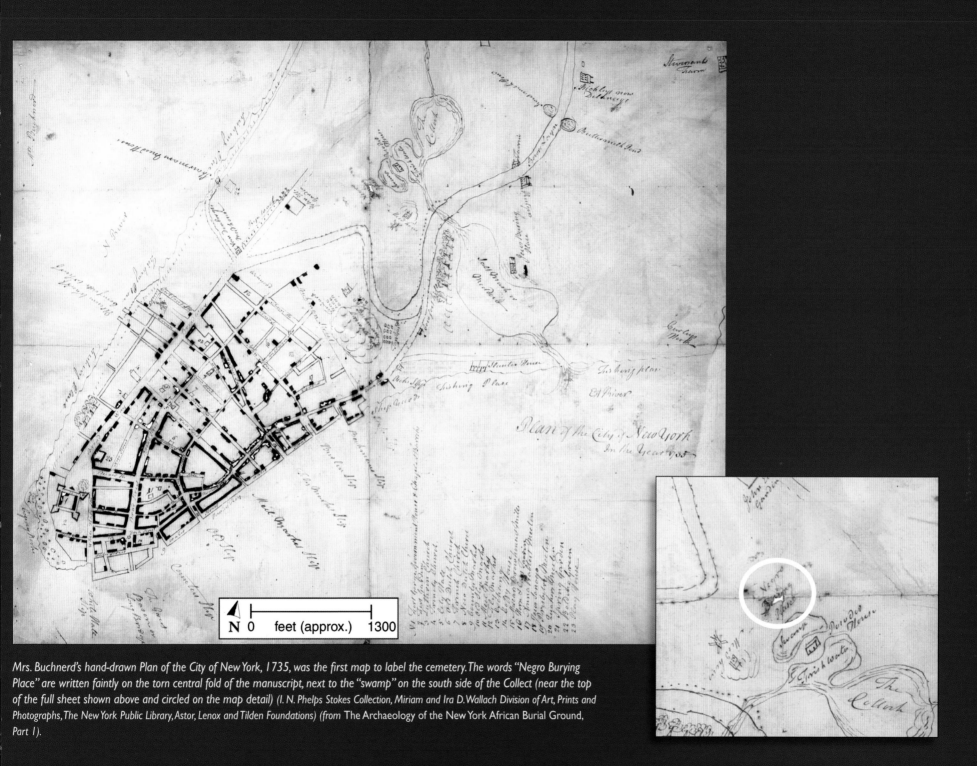

Mrs. Buchnerd's hand-drawn *Plan of the City of New York*, 1735, was the first map to label the cemetery. The words "Negro Burying Place" are written faintly on the torn central fold of the manuscript, next to the "swamp" on the south side of the Collect (near the top of the full sheet shown above and circled on the map detail) (I. N. Phelps Stokes Collection, Miriam and Ira D. Wallach Division of Art, Prints and Photographs, The New York Public Library, Astor, Lenox and Tilden Foundations) (from *The Archaeology of the New York African Burial Ground, Part 1*).

During the 1700s, many Africans attended Trinity Church services. Eight-hundred-sixty-nine Africans were baptized at Trinity Church between 1704 and 1764, but very few were allowed to be church members. Trinity Church established a small, separate burial ground for Africans in 1773 located between present-day Church Street, Reade Street, and West Broadway. Like the African Burial Ground, this burial ground was used until 1795. Because burial records have not been located, it is not possible to know who was buried there.

The Closing of the African Burial Ground

By the late 1780s, survey of new lots in Calk Hook Farm prevented use of the northernmost part of the burial ground. The area available for burial became smaller and smaller over the next decade. African New Yorkers petitioned the city in 1794 for a new burial ground. The next year, the city gave £100 toward the purchase of a 0.23-acre plot on Chrystie Street. Isaac Fortune and the African Society for Mutual Aid convinced the city to give them rights to this property. Africans developed the property, managed the burial grounds, and collected burial fees. That same year, the Van Borsum patent was divided into 67 lots, leaving no place for burial in this part of the burial ground.

By the end of the 1700s, a yellow fever epidemic caused panic in the city. To prevent disease, areas around the Collect Pond were cleared of waste and debris, and standing water was drained. Burials were no longer allowed within the city because officials feared that decaying dead bodies would spread disease. Several hundred Africans who died from the epidemic were buried in the potter's field at Washington Square. Another 41 were buried at the new African cemetery on Chrystie Street.

A few years later, the Collect Pond and portions of the burial ground were filled in and leveled off with as much as 25 feet of dirt. Covering the burial ground with dirt preserved many burials. Otherwise, they would have been disturbed by building construction. Around the same time, African Zion Church was prevented from using a vault beneath the church for burial. In response, the church acquired burial space in the potter's field at West Fourth Street, just outside Washington Square Park.

Used for well over a century, the African Burial Ground may have contained as many as 15,000 burials. Even after it was covered over, African Americans kept a watchful eye on the areas where their loved ones were buried. The spirit of the African Burial Ground lived on through new African American institutions in Manhattan, such as the city's first African American churches and mutual aid societies. Covered for many generations, the African Burial Ground is a reminder of the early and vital history of Africans in New York.

Isaac Fortune
William Hutson
James Parker
John Hall
Abraham
    Dickenson
Peter Frances

Detail of a petition submitted in June 1795 by the African Society requesting that six of its members be granted legal standing to manage the Chrystie Street cemetery established for black New Yorkers. The names of the proposed managers are marked with a check (courtesy New York Municipal Archives; Papers of the Common Council, Petitions [Isaac Fortune, June 19, 1795]) (from The Archaeology of the New York African Burial Ground, Part 1*).*

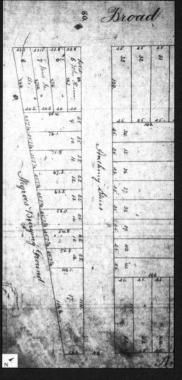

Detail from a 1787 surveyor's map showing the partition of the Calk Hook Farm into lots. The lots on the southern side of Anthony Street (present-day Duane), shown to the right of the "Negroes Burying Ground," actually overlapped the cemetery's n orthern edge. Broadway crosses at the top of the map detail. Ann (present-day Elk) Street crosses at the bottom. Lot dimensions are shown in feet (courtesy of the Division of Land Records [Liber 46:140]).

Detail from the Taylor-Roberts Plan, 1797, drawn by city surveyor Benjamin Taylor and engraved by John Roberts, showing the newly laid street grid that crossed the African Burial Ground at the end of the eighteenth century (The Lionel Pincus and Princess Firyal Map Division, The New York Public Library, Astor, Lenox and Tilden Foundations).

Both images from The Archaeology of the New York African Burial Ground, Part 1.

Archaeological Periods of Burial Ground Use

Archaeologists used historical and archaeological evidence to place burials in time. Historical-period fence lines and landownership showed which areas of the burial ground could have been used at different times. Trash from the pottery and tannery in some graves suggests the graves were dug during or after the time the trash was deposited (ca. 1728–1765). Artifacts that could be dated, such as coins, were used in a similar fashion. It makes sense that a burial with a dated artifact could not have been placed before the artifact was made, so it has to date to a time after the artifact was produced. The arrangement of burials was also used to suggest when burials were placed in time relative to each other. Burials beneath other burials must have been placed earlier than the burials above them. In addition, change in coffin shape over time was used to determine when a burial might have been placed.

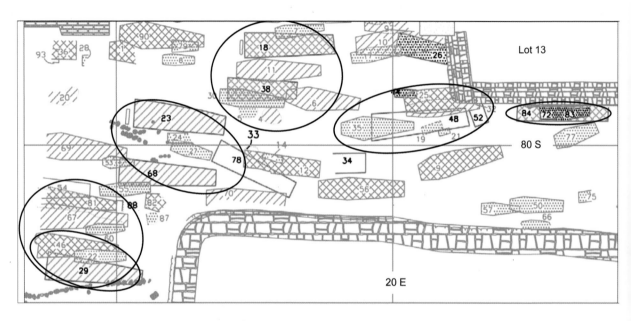

Together, all these facts allowed archaeologists to define four time periods of use for the cemetery. Based on when they were thought to have been buried, individuals were placed in temporal groups defined by a date span. For example, the Early Group burials date between the time the burial ground began to be used to before 1735, when trash was first dumped on the burial ground by local industries. Fifty-two burials were placed in the Early Group. The next group, called the Middle Group, dated between 1735 and 1760 and contained 198 burials. This group is larger because some burials of uncertain age were placed in this group. The Late-Middle Group dated between 1760 and 1776. Changes in land use were important in defining this group. Because houses or fences were built in areas of the burial ground during the 1760s, it was determined that burials were probably not placed there and were forced into other areas of the burial ground. The final group, called the Late Group, dated from the Revolutionary War to the closing of the burial ground (1776–1795).

Archaeologists used these groups to study how the burial ground was used through time. Based on the number of burials found to belong to each period, the excavated area of the burial ground was most heavily used after 1735. Use appears to have been heaviest

Detail of the southwestern portion of the site plan showing all temporal groups. Early Group burials are shown in color, and possible clusters are circled. Later burials are shown in gray (from The Archaeology of the New York African Burial Ground, *Part I).*

44

Coins

Three individuals were buried with coins over their eyes at the New York African Burial Ground: two women (Burials 230 and 242) and one man (Burial 135). All were adults between 30 and 65 years old. A 55–65-year-old woman (Burial 230) was buried with two cast copper-alloy coins of different sizes. The larger coin was found near her left eye and could have slipped out when she was buried. The location of the smaller coin was not recorded, but bits of textile were attached to both sides. The coin might have slipped from her right eye into the burial clothes or rested inside a pocket or a cloth purse buried with the woman. The two cast copper coins found with a 40–50-year-old woman (Burial 242) remained in her eye sockets. A man who was 30–40 years old (Burial 135) had one copper coin above his right shoulder, which could have fallen from the right eye socket. The other remained in his left eye socket. Hair and cloth were noted on the coins. The coin from the left eye socket was X-rayed at the Metropolitan Museum of Art and found to be a George II halfpenny, dating between 1727 and 1760.

Copper coin (George II halfpenny) from Burial 135 (photograph by Jon Abbott).

The New York African Burial Ground researchers placed these burials with copper coins in the Late Group (1776–1795), in part because the burials must have taken place after these coins were made. Although the sample of burials with coins was small, the coins were found only in burials of older adults assigned to the Late Group. Based on these findings, the New York African Burial Ground researchers suggest that placing coins on the eyes of the dead might have been a practice used toward the later part of the eighteenth century. This custom might also have been set aside to honor older individuals.

X-rayed copper George II halfpenny from Burial 135 and 1749 George II halfpenny from University of Notre Dame Libraries.

All images from The Archaeology of the New York African Burial Ground, Part 1.

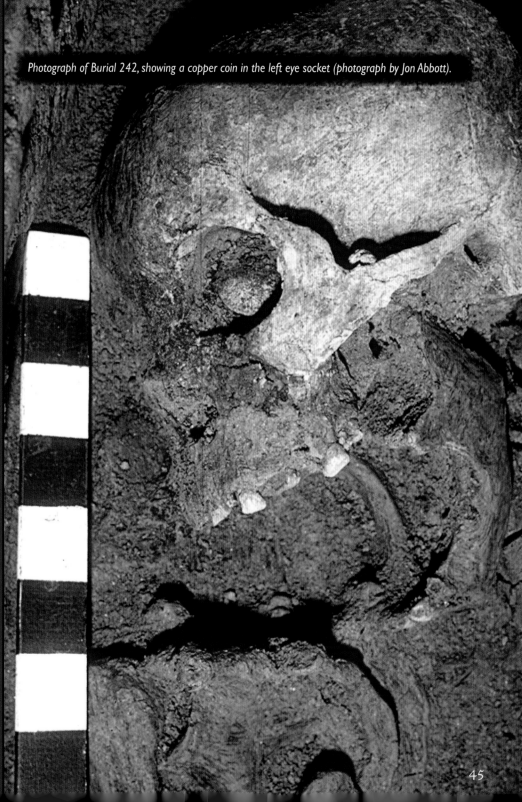

Photograph of Burial 242, showing a copper coin in the left eye socket (photograph by Jon Abbott).

between 1735 and 1760 and again between 1776 and 1795. Use may have been lighter between 1760 and 1776 because of building construction and the fencing of a portion of the burial ground. Change in burial treatment was also studied using temporal groups. Coffin shapes changed over time: the earliest coffins were rectangular or tapered in shape, and later ones were hexagonal. A number of burials in the Late Group were without coffins. This is probably because many Africans were new in the city during the Revolutionary War, and persons buried without coffins might not have family or friends in the city to look after their burial and provide a coffin.

Temporal groupings could also be used to compare skeletal data with historical census data. For instance, census data suggest that close to equal numbers of African men and women lived in the city throughout much of the 1700s. During some periods, there were more African women than men. Skeletal data tell a different tale, as there were almost twice as many men as women in the burial ground during some periods. This could suggest that there were more African men in the city than were reported, or African men died at higher rates than African women, or this area of the burial ground was used more often for burying males. Finally, the temporal period of the burial was used to study change in identity. An adult male aged 26–35 with modified teeth (Burial 101) buried after 1776 had what may be an Akan/Asante symbol on the coffin. Shaped like a heart, the symbol was made with tacks on his coffin lid. Although the design could have been Christian, the use of the symbol could mean that African identities remained strong in colonial New York, even toward the end of the 1700s. Africans were constantly arriving in Manhattan, renewing knowledge and traditions from African homelands among the enslaved. Thus, for those who were enslaved, African identities were not lost but remained strong through time.

Coffin Burial

Burial in a coffin was considered part of a proper burial in colonial New York. The use of coffins differs from traditional African practice before the 1700s, when most people were wrapped in cloth or mats. Coffins did come into use in Africa through exposure to European practices. Coffins would not have been foreign to African New Yorkers. The use of coffins could reflect common Christian practice, the provision of coffins by enslavers, or health concerns. In the African Burial Ground, 353 of the 385 graves for which the presence or absence of a coffin could be determined contained coffins (91.7 percent).

When the African Burial Ground was used, English society regarded the coffin as an essential part of a decent funeral. Even the poor were provided coffins. At the time, cities like London, New York, and Paris were crowded and unsanitary. City dwellers lived under constant fear of infectious diseases. In the late 1700s, New Yorkers feared that corpses spread disease and may have used coffins to prevent epidemics. Given the cost of coffins, it seems likely that providing them was the responsibility of enslavers. The preparation of the body, the placement of grave goods, and the ceremonies and rituals of burial seem to have been left to the mourners.

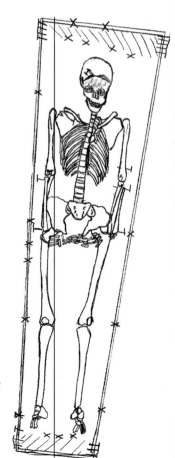

Left, *Drawing of Burial 35* (drawing by T. Gray); right, *Drawing of Burial 23* (drawing by C.S.G.) (from The Archaeology of the New York African Burial Ground, *Part 2*).

Burial 101

Burial 101 had a heart-shaped symbol hammered into the coffin lid with 187 tacks. Possible initials, which were unreadable, and the year "1769" were hammered with tacks inside the heart shape. Europeans used similar symbols on coffins of the time, but at least one West African symbol is also similar. This is the Akan Sankofa symbol, which means "It is not a taboo to return and fetch it when you forget." Sankofa reminds people to tie the present with the past in order to prepare for the future. Because it was similar to a commonly used European symbol, mourners may have used the Sankofa symbol as a way to signal African identity without calling attention to the symbol's true meaning.

The 26-35-year-old man in Burial 101 was an unusual individual in terms of mortuary treatment; perhaps he had complex origins. Use of the symbol and teeth modified by chipping and filing would suggest West African origins. However, other evidence suggests he may not have been born in West Africa. For instance, the strontium isotope signature in his teeth was similar to someone who had grown up in New York rather than in West Africa. He could possibly have come from a place with strontium isotope signatures similar to those of New York, such as southern Africa or some area of the Americas. Trace elements also did not clearly link the man with West Africa, although low lead levels suggest this man may not have lived in New York for long. It is possible that, if he was not from West Africa, he could have affiliated himself with the Akan through kinship. The Akan were especially powerful and active in the New York area in colonial times.

Possible reading of the year "1769" formed by tacks on the lid of Burial 101 (drawing by M. Schur).

One version of the West African Sankofa symbol.

Coffin lid decoration formed of iron tacks in Burial 101 (photograph by Dennis Seckler).

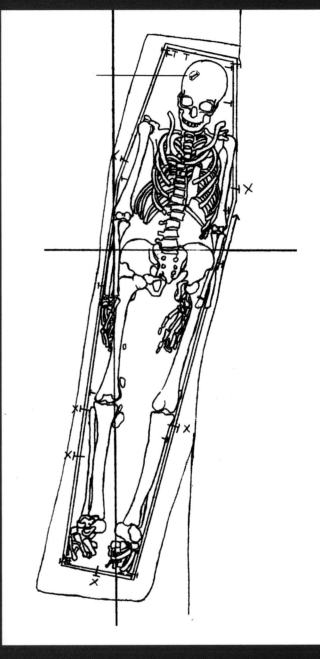

Drawing of skeletal remains in Burial 101 (drawing by M. Schur).

ORIGINS

Africa, a huge continent, contains one-fifth of all the land mass in the world. More than three times larger than the United States, Africa has more than 50 countries. It is also home to hundreds of different cultures, and about 2,000 different languages are spoken there. In short, Africa is vast and diverse.

To say simply that someone came from Africa ignores the diversity of this great continent. Europeans, however, came to see all people of African descent as a race, as "Negroes" or "black" people. As their contact with other parts of the world increased, Europeans also came to view people of European descent, or "whites," as a superior race. Europeans in seventeenth-century Manhattan believed that the Africans in their midst were less important and less accomplished than themselves based solely on racial differences. This perception, which we now know as racism, led them to justify denying enslaved Africans the right to have or do what was allowed to other people in the land. It also led them to force enslaved Africans to work for others, to oppress them and deprive them of the bare essentials, and to ridicule and subject them to brutal punishments.

Today the concept of race has been proven false, but the false racial concepts and racism that we Americans live with today came about during the time that the African Burial Ground was in use. These views have hidden the real history of African New Yorkers: where they came from, what they endured, and what they accomplished. Before the African Burial Ground Project, many scientists studied people of African descent using racialized theories that have since been discredited.

Importations of Central Africans into the Americas, 1601–1800

Years	Total No. of Individuals Imported from Central Africa	Total No. of Individuals Imported to the Atlantic Region	Percentage of Central African Individuals
1601–1650	564,700	608,800	92.8
1651–1675	88,400	223,500	39.6
1676–1700	134,100	516,300	26.0
1701–1725	256,700	956,300	26.8
1726–1750	550,400	1,303,700	42.2
1751–1775	712,000	1,901,200	37.4
1776–1800	813,900	1,906,000	42.7

Note: From Miller (2002:67). This table originally appeared in *Historical Perspectives of the African Burial Ground: New York Blacks and the Diaspora.*

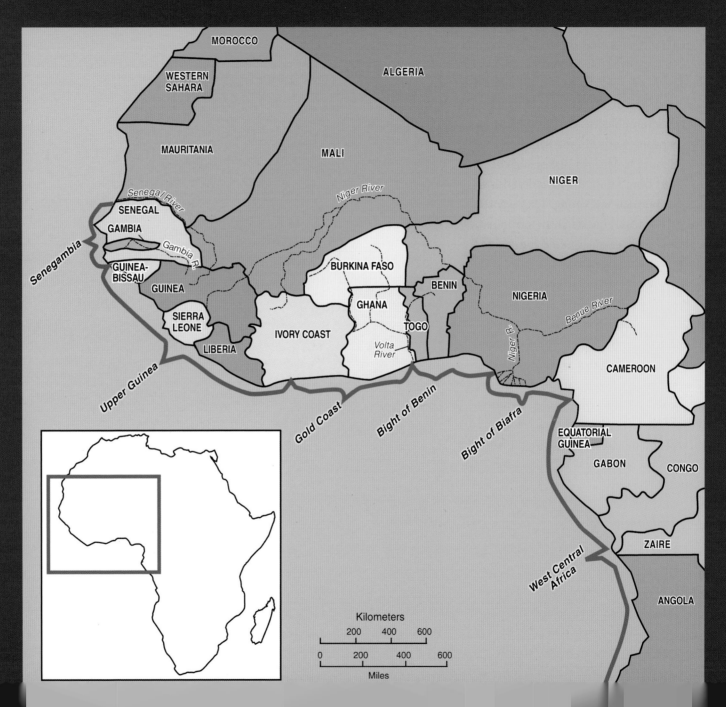

The map to the right shows how the major regions of Africa from the seventeenth and eighteenth centuries correspond to modern countries. The regions were exit points for enslaved individuals bound for New York during the time the African Burial Ground was in use. Additional exit points (not shown) include Mozambique and western Madagascar as well as the Atlantic islands off of West Africa (e.g., Cape Verde) (from The Skeletal Biology of the New York African Burial Ground, Part 1).

They did not view the Africans who were enslaved in the Americas and the Caribbean as people from different parts of Africa who brought the knowledge and practice of different cultures with them to the New World. They used a few African groups to represent all people from Africa and ignored Africa's rich and diverse histories and cultures.

Some anthropologists wanted to use race to study people buried in the African Burial Ground, but Dr. Michael Blakey and the researchers from Howard University insisted that this approach was wrong. They wanted to study the people buried at the site in terms of the deceased person's specific cultures and history. By doing so, they hoped to learn the real story of where these people came from and how they once led their lives in Africa, the Caribbean, and New York. To find this information, Dr. Blakey and his team used a biocultural approach that takes into account the areas the people came from, the languages they spoke, and other historical and cultural information. Only this approach, they believed, could help us to understand who the people buried at the New York African Burial Ground really were.

African Homelands

The relocation of Africans to other parts of the world, such as the Americas, led to the creation of an African Diaspora. A diaspora includes a people's homeland and any new area to which they disperse, whether by force or voluntarily. In the case of the African Diaspora, the movement of African people was forced. By the mid-1800s, more than

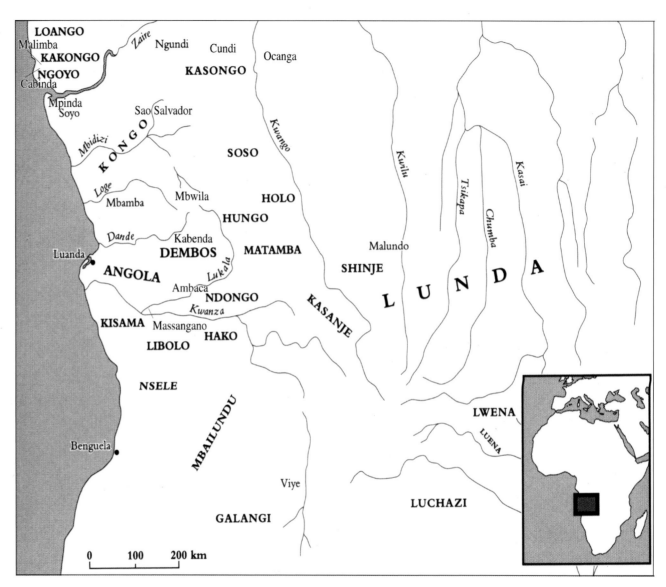

West Central Africa, Kongo-Angola Region. As the researchers note in Historical Perspectives of the African Burial Ground, "The principal area that provided enslaved Africans to New Amsterdam stretched over 720 miles along the Atlantic from the port of Mpinda in the north, Luanda in the center, and Benguela in the south and then inland for approximately 240 miles." During the 1700s, enslaved Africans from West Central Africa were transported from the interior to coastal settlements like Malimba, Cabinda, Luanda, and Benguela, where they were "sold" to European slavers. (Adapted from Warfare in Atlantic Africa, 1500–1800, John Thornton, ©1999, UCL Press. Reproduced by permission of Taylor & Francis Books UK.) (From Historical Perspectives of the African Burial Ground..)

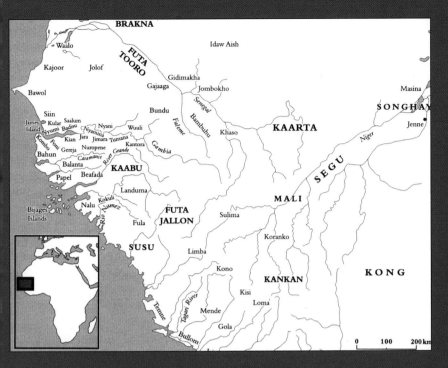

The Senegambia Region, West Africa.

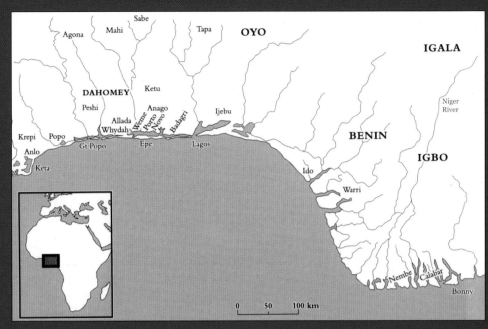

The Bight of Benin and Niger Delta, West Africa.

The black community of New York was enlarged by imports of enslaved laborers from West Africa in the mid-1600s as West Africans became the largest African group imported into New York. The regions from which the West Africans originated consisted of five areas: the Senegambia, the Sierra Leone–Liberia region, the Gold Coast, the Bight of Benin, and the Niger Delta. (The three maps on this page were adapted from Warfare in Atlantic Africa, 1500–1800, John Thornton, ©1999, UCL Press. Reproduced by permission of Taylor & Francis Books UK.) (All images on this page are from Historical Perspectives of the African Burial Ground.)

The Gold Coast and Slave Coast, West Africa.

11 million Africans had been kidnapped from their homelands and enslaved in the Americas and the Caribbean. This created one of the largest and most tragic diasporas in world history.

Enslaved Africans came from many different societies on their native continent. They also had a wide range of skills and life experiences. They spoke diverse languages and had different customs and beliefs. Some of the people taken were from huge and powerful kingdoms, like the Kongo of Angola, but many others lived in small communities. Many were farmers or herders. Others fished the rivers and the ocean. Some made cloth, created ceramic pots, mined for gold, or made metal tools for a living. Others were soldiers, porters, traders, or community leaders. Because Europeans were active along the African coast for centuries, many Africans knew about the foreigners' languages, customs, and religious practices. They also knew about the European goods, such as guns and other armaments, that were traded for gold, ivory, and enslaved Africans.

Most enslaved Africans landed in the Caribbean and South America. The largest number was sent to Brazil to work on huge plantations. Smaller numbers were imported to North American colonies such as New York. Many of those Africans were sent first to the Caribbean before being shipped to New York. They often came from Senegambia, the Ivory Coast and Ghana, and the Bight of Benin area. More than half of African New Yorkers who arrived in Manhattan directly from Africa were from Senegambia. The Akan, or West African people known as Coromantees, were also common in New York. Some African New Yorkers were Malagasy from Madagascar, an island in southeast Africa, who were acquired illegally from pirates at a lower cost than other Africans.

Studying Origins with Bones and Teeth

The New York African Burial Ground Project researchers used many methods to study the origins of the Africans buried at that site. Historians and anthropologists studied the regions where the Africans came from, focusing on beliefs and customs, diet, and work. They studied how people from each region were enslaved and brought to the Americas. To better understand what the enslaved Africans went through in the Caribbean before coming to New York, researchers also studied life in the Caribbean.

Skeletal biologists studied bones and teeth to learn where the deceased came from. They compared the shapes of the human skulls (or crania) and teeth excavated from the site to see how similar they were to those of Europeans, Native Americans, and people from different parts of Africa. They compared DNA from bones to DNA

African Origins

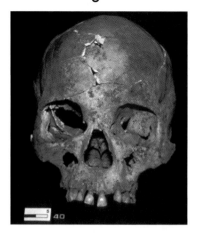
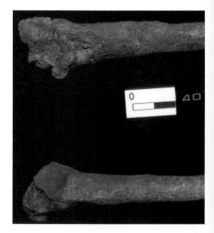

Through molecular genetic testing, this elderly woman 50–60 years of age (Burial 40) (left) was determined to be from the Niger region of West Africa. Researchers determined her origins by analyzing DNA extracted from her calf bone (right) (from The Skeletal Biology of the New York African Burial Ground, *Part 1).*

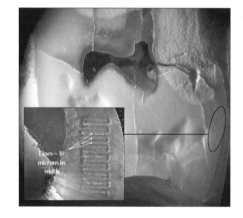

Advanced analytical techniques were used to determine the African origins of the people at the New York African Burial Ground. Researchers compared trace elements in tooth tissue from these individuals with trace element profiles of West African teeth. Trace elements are incorporated into the hard tissues of teeth when a person has lived in an area for a long time or regularly eats particular foods. Extremely thin sections of each tooth (see section of upper right first molar from Burial 23, left) were sliced with a diamond-coated copper blade. Tissue was then extracted in a "raster pattern" (see inset, far left). As a result of this analysis, researchers determined that the 25–35-year-old man in Burial 23 was of African birth. His teeth (the central incisors) had been modified to a wedge shape, a practice known in Congo, southwest Angola, and southeast Africa (from The Skeletal Biology of the New York African Burial Ground, *Part 1).*

Kongo woman laboring in agricultural field (courtesy *of University of Arizona Special Collections, from* Relation historique de l'Ethiopie occidentale; contenant la description des royaumes de Congo, Angolle et Matamba, *by Giovanni Cavazzi, 1732) (from* Historical Perspectives of the African Burial Ground).

53

from living Africans and African Americans. They compared levels of trace elements and isotopes in teeth to expected levels for different parts of Africa, the Caribbean, and New York. New York African Burial Ground Project researchers studied the teeth of skeletons unearthed from the burial ground to determine how old the people were when they were forced into slavery. They studied isotopes and trace elements in teeth to learn when in life a person moved from one place to another. These studies determined whether a person was born in Africa or New York or was first sent to the Caribbean before being sent to New York.

In one experiment, the researchers selected a sample of individuals with modified teeth, a cultural practice known in Africa, and analyzed their teeth for strontium isotopes. They compared their findings with the results from the same tests performed on the teeth of children buried at the burial ground, and the results indicated that many people buried in the burial ground were from West and West Central Africa. Others, particularly children, were probably born in the Caribbean or in New York. Researchers also found that Africans in New York came from many different societies in that continent.

One of the challenges the New York African Burial Ground Project researchers faced with these studies was related to the lack of data on specific groups of African people. Part of this problem comes from previous studies that focused on studying Africans as a race. In the past, small numbers of Africans from different parts of Africa were used to represent all Africans. This approach ignores the many differences between Africans and the changes over time that have taken place among African groups.

A better approach, the project researchers decided, would be to compare people from the New York African Burial Ground to African groups from specific times

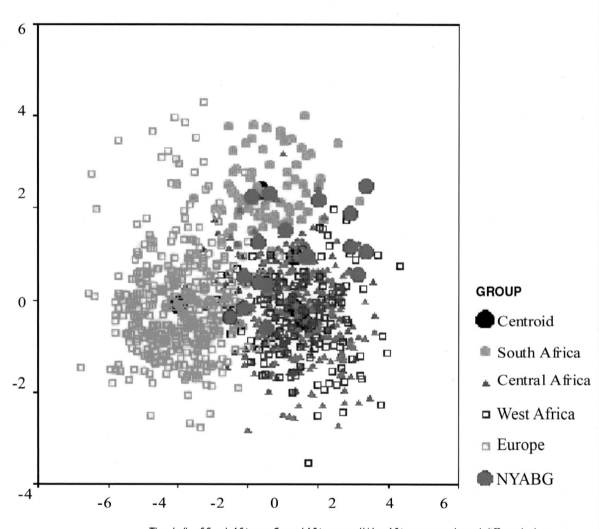

New York African Burial Ground Skull Shape Analysis

GROUP

● Centroid

▦ South Africa

▲ Central Africa

□ West Africa

▫ Europe

⬡ NYABG

The skulls of South Africans, Central Africans, and West Africans were shaped differently than the skulls of Europeans. The shape of the skulls from the New York African Burial Ground was similar to those of other Africans and differed from those of Europeans. Note how the New York African Burial Ground population (red dots) overlapped with sample populations from West Africa (blue squares), Central Africa (pink triangles), and South Africa (orange-brown dots) (from The Skeletal Biology of the New York African Burial Ground, *Part 1).*

Ethnohistory

The historical and anthropological study of specific ethnic groups is called ethnohistory. Ethnohistoric research on many different African groups was needed to understand the specific backgrounds of the African New Yorkers buried at the New York African Burial Ground. One of the difficulties faced by the project researchers was the lack of accurate information on West and West Central African groups whose members were enslaved and sent to New York City. Another problem was the fact that most studies of African cultures were done hundreds of years after enslavement took place. Those studies do not describe what Africans did and thought during the 1600s and 1700s. Instead, they reflect conditions in Africa in the 1800s and 1900s, after many significant cultural changes took place. The early histories are also extremely biased and generally convey Europeans' most negative and limited views of Africans. Europeans failed to understand the differences between groups or the reasons behind African practices that were foreign to them.

The New York African Burial Ground Project researchers combined historical accounts, information from modern ethnographies of West and West Central groups, and archaeological evidence to develop a better understanding of African cultures during the 1600s and 1700s. Unfortunately, much research has focused on writings in English, when many historical accounts are written in Portuguese, French, or Dutch. During the course of their historical research, New York African Burial Ground Project historians consulted accounts written in other languages and were able to draw information on West Central Africa from Portuguese sources. As more historians begin to research these other sources of historical information, even more knowledge on African beliefs and customs is likely to follow.

Trace Elements and Isotopes

Elements that occur naturally in very small amounts in soil, plant, and wildlife (known as trace elements) are distinctive of particular geographic regions. When a person lives in an area for a long time, trace elements are incorporated into bones and teeth as the individual grows and develops. Researchers use this information, stored in bones and teeth, to learn where a person lived at different points in their life. By comparing levels of trace elements found in teeth to levels found in food and water in different regions, researchers can learn where a person may have lived. Depending on when they grew during a person's lifetime, different areas of individual teeth, as well as different teeth from the same individual, can be used to develop a chronology of places where a person may have lived over the course of his or her lifetime.

Isotope ratios of the metal strontium (Sr) are also distinctive for geographic regions. Isotopes are different types of atoms of the same chemical element that have the same number of protons but a different number of neutrons. The ratio of one strontium isotope (^{86}Sr) to another (^{87}Sr), as measured in soil, water, and organisms, differs between different parts of the world. In the same manner as with trace elements, researchers can learn whether the strontium found in teeth was absorbed in Africa, New York, or some other area.

New York African Burial Ground Project researchers studied isotope and trace element signatures in teeth to learn who among the people buried at the site grew up in the New York area, somewhere in Africa, or in the Caribbean. The researchers also used this information to learn at what ages children were enslaved and brought to New York.

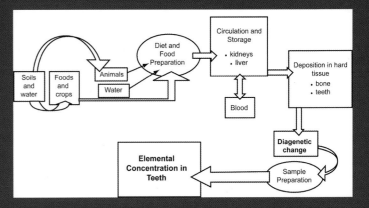

Model showing how chemical elements are deposited in teeth (from The Skeletal Biology of the New York African Burial Ground, *Part 1).*

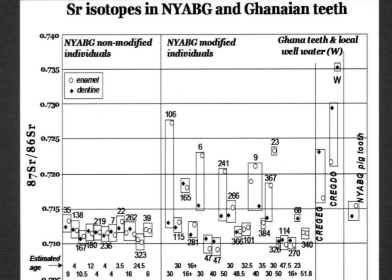

^{87}Strontium to ^{86}Strontium ratios in samples of enamel and dentine of individuals from the New York African Burial Ground, plus two individuals from Ghana; water from Ghana; and an intrusive pig molar (from The Skeletal Biology of the New York African Burial Ground, *Part 1).*

and places. To do this, the researchers studied the archaeology and history of groups living in the areas where the buried African New Yorkers were born. They also began building a database of African DNA that currently is being used to help African Americans learn where in Africa their ancestors came from. They are also calling for better collections of skeletons from different groups in Africa, which would help scientists to compare those skeletons with the remains of the people buried in the New York African Burial Ground.

How Africans Were Enslaved

Slavery occurred in both Africa and the Americas, but it was not the same in both places. In Africa, Africans enslaved by other Africans could own property, petition authorities, and be freed. They could also work for themselves and hold positions of high authority. Sometimes, they were treated like family members and became spouses or adopted children. Enslaved women were highly valued for child care, farming, and skills in making cloth or pottery.

Once the Atlantic slave trade was started, the American demand for enslaved laborers caused major unrest in West and West Central Africa. Africans who were captured as prisoners of war by powerful states like that of the Asante of Ghana and others who violated customs, owed a debt, or were simply accused of committing a crime were given over to the European and American enslavers. Some were kidnapped as they walked to their fields. Many wars for power and captives were fought. African males were often enslaved as soldiers in wars to enslave others. Entire villages were raided for captives. The few Africans who benefited from the slave trade were powerful elites and traders. Countless lives were destroyed because of the Atlantic slave trade, perhaps several times more than the number of people who were actually enslaved.

Once captured, the enslaved Africans were given little food or water, and many were probably injured. They were forced to walk many miles to the coast and were beaten along the way. At the coast, captive Africans were held in cramped spaces at forts and other places to await sale, where European and American slave traders arrived in ships to "purchase" enslaved Africans and take them away. Some European powers, like the Portuguese and the British, had forts along the coast to purchase captured Africans. Others, like the French, sailed along the coast and stopped where they could find enslaved Africans for sale.

Dental Modification

Dental modification is the practice of filing down, removing, or breaking chips from teeth to change their appearance. Long ago, some Native American groups practiced dental modification. During the 1600s and 1700s, many African groups practiced dental modification in Africa. During special ceremonies that marked the passage of individuals into new stages in life, their teeth were modified into many shapes, including pegs, hourglass shapes, points, and other shapes. Despite the use of distinctive forms of modification, it is not possible at this time to link a specific kind of dental modification with a specific group. Many of the kinds of dental modification that are currently known were performed in the Congo region of West Central Africa. They were also practiced in the Gold Coast of West Africa and areas of southeast Africa.

Because enslaved Africans were removed from settings where dental modification was performed, many archaeologists believe that enslaved Africans with modified teeth living in the Americas were born in Africa and would not have modified their teeth while living in the Americas. The New York African Burial Ground Project researchers also assumed that adults with modified teeth were African born.

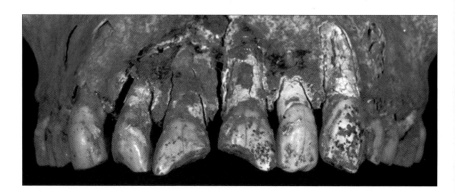

Example of dental modification of maxillary central incisors (from The Skeletal Biology of the New York African Burial Ground, *Part 1).*

Burial 340

Different lines of evidence suggest that the 39–64-year-old woman in Burial 340 was born in Africa and retained aspects of her African heritage while living in Manhattan. The woman in Burial 340 had teeth that had been worked into hourglass and peg shapes, an African practice. Studies of trace elements and strontium isotopes in her teeth, along with low lead levels, confirm the woman in Burial 340 was probably of African birth. Artifacts also suggest connections to Africa. She wore a strand of beads around her waist that was characteristic of African practices and included one bead made in Africa.

The strand was made of 112 glass beads, 1 amber bead, and 7 cowries. Another set of alternating blue and yellow beads was either part of a bracelet or was part of the waist strand. Historical records note that strings of hip beads in some West African societies were used to keep garments secure and hide a woman's figure. Most beads found with her were made in Europe, but one amber bead was probably made in Africa.

The waist strand was also decorated with cowry shells. The British and the Dutch shipped more than 25 million pounds of cowries into West African ports between 1700 and 1790. Most were from East Africa or the Maldive Islands in the Indian Ocean. Cowries were used like money over much of West Africa. Few cowries or beads survived the journey across the Atlantic, and were usually seized by enslavers. Burial 340 somehow kept hers.

All images on this page are from The Archaeology of the New York African Burial Ground, *Part 1.*

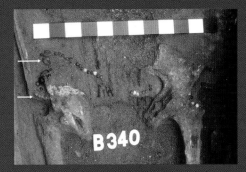

Photograph of Burial 340, showing beads. The top arrow points to one of the cowries, the bottom arrow to the strand of alternating blue-green and yellow beads at the right wrist (see drawing of the beads in place on Page 91) (photograph by Dennis Seckler).

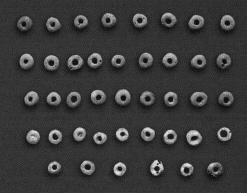

Translucent blue-green and opaque beads from Burial 340 (photograph by Jon Abbott).

Deep blue beads from Burial 340 (photograph by Jon Abbott).

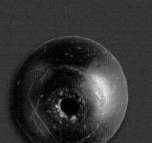

Simple black bead from Burial 340 (photograph by Jon Abbott).

Possibly translucent amber beads from Burial 340 that developed a coating over time (photograph by Jon Abbott).

Decorated and amber beads from Burial 340 (photograph by Jon Abbott).

Cowry shell from Burial 340 (photograph by Jon Abbott).

The Middle Passage

The journey of captives from Africa to the Americas is known as the Middle Passage. The enslaved Africans were packed into ships' holds like logs, some nursing injuries from when they were captured or beaten. Sick with worry, fear, and sadness, they had been torn away from their loved ones and taken from their homelands. Bound and shackled, beaten, deprived of food and water, and humiliated, they had lost everything and did not know where their lives were heading. Given little food or water, they were beaten when considered rebellious. They developed sores from being packed into cramped spaces and became sick from diseases that spread quickly in close quarters. Many were shackled for long periods of the journey, although in some cases, women and children were free to move about once the ship was underway. Men were rarely allowed on deck, because they were considered a threat.

To escape a life of slavery, some African captives jumped overboard into shark-infested waters. An estimated 13 percent of enslaved Africans died on the way to American ports. On some voyages, nearly all died of disease or malnutrition.

For those Africans who survived the Middle Passage, the effects of the voyage and the life of slavery that followed caused major health problems. Scientists know that breaks or gaps in enamel can show when in life a person was diseased or malnourished. Therefore, the New York African Burial Ground Project researchers studied enamel on the teeth of the deceased Africans recovered at the site to learn when these individuals had serious health problems during their lifetimes. Studies of teeth suggested that enslavement and the Middle Passage destroyed the health of people, some of whom had been fairly healthy in Africa before being enslaved. Those who were enslaved in New York as children had frequent health problems, and those problems may have started when the children were taken from their parents and put to work. Many of the enslaved Africans who died between 15 and 24 years of age also had health problems as children. The Middle Passage was probably a major cause of health problems for the people in that group. Those who had been enslaved as adults had fewer health problems in childhood than those enslaved at younger ages.

Shipborne Trade

During the 1700s, the shipborne slave trade, or "coasting," was common in the Ivory Coast, Liberia, the Niger Delta, and Sierra Leone. Shipborne trade was a particular method of trade that did not involve established trading posts or forts. Captives were instead acquired in coastal towns and cities whenever and wherever they were available. According to this method, European slave ships traveled along the coast of West Africa or West Central Africa, purchasing or bartering for enslaved Africans at one or two stops along the way. In Lower Guinea—from the western Ivory Coast to Cameroon—British, French, and Dutch ships usually drew enslaved Africans from two stops. In the Senegambia region and on the Angola Coast of West Central Africa, one stop was more common. The few stops made by a single vessel meant that Africans on a single voyage were often from some of the same areas in Africa and had similar ethnic backgrounds.

Forts

In 1482, the Portuguese established the Castelo de São Jorge da Mina along the Gold Coast, in present-day Ghana. Later known simply as Elmina, the castle and settlement became a major center for the trade in enslaved Africans. The Portuguese built smaller forts on the Gold Coast at Axim, Shama, and Accra. At first, the Portuguese traded for luxury items, such as spices, ivory, and gold. Over time, the Portuguese, Dutch, and English fought for control of Elmina as the demand for enslaved Africans increased. Europeans eventually built around 60 forts along the coast of West Africa to support the trade in enslaved Africans, most of them concentrated along the Gold Coast. Africans from vast areas of the interior were held at such forts before being sold to European enslavers. Many enslaved Africans had similar backgrounds, as they were taken from the same regions during military campaigns. In the Americas, Europeans often identified the ethnic background of enslaved Africans based on the port where the enslaved were acquired. Akan-speaking Africans from the Gold Coast, for instance, were often called "Mina," in reference to Elmina.

A Liverpool Slave Ship About 1780, by William Jackson (© National Museums Liverpool [The International Slavery Museum]).

Life in the Caribbean

Most African New Yorkers were first shipped to the Caribbean, where enslaved men, women, and children were pressed into hard labor on sugar plantations, working from dawn to dusk. There, they dug countless holes to plant crops by hand, tended fields, cared for livestock, and brought in the harvest. They also worked in the mills to make sugar from cane. They were constantly lifting and pulling, pushing, stooping, and straining their muscles to perform the many chores forced upon them.

Then, after working the fields and mills all day, they had to work to ensure their own survival. Planters gave them little food to eat, so the Africans grew much of their own food themselves. After long days in the sun, they ground corn and cooked it into a gruel to eat with a little salted fish. Sleep was precious, but small, dark huts with damp, dirt floors were their only resting places. Sickness was common, and many Africans died after a few years or even a few months under such conditions. To keep the African population from dying out, enslavers needed new laborers on a regular basis.

In the Caribbean, Africans lived together in large groups, away from the plantation owners' and overseers' homes. They used African methods to build their houses, plant gardens, make pots and baskets, and cook meals. As most were from the same areas in Africa, their African backgrounds were not lost in these places but strengthened. They shared songs and stories from their homelands, nursed the sick, and plotted against their enslavers. They also greatly outnumbered the Euroamericans on the islands, who used brutal force to control the population. Open rebellion was common.

Enslavers called Africans who had spent some time in the Caribbean "seasoned." Seasoned Africans were more highly valued by New York colonists than were "unseasoned" laborers direct from Africa. They were more familiar with European languages and had survived disease, psychological trauma, and hard labor. However, of the Africans sent to New York from the Caribbean, many were disabled, hard to control, or aged. Caribbean enslavers were willing to give these individuals up to New York enslavers, who were unable to afford "prime" seasoned laborers.

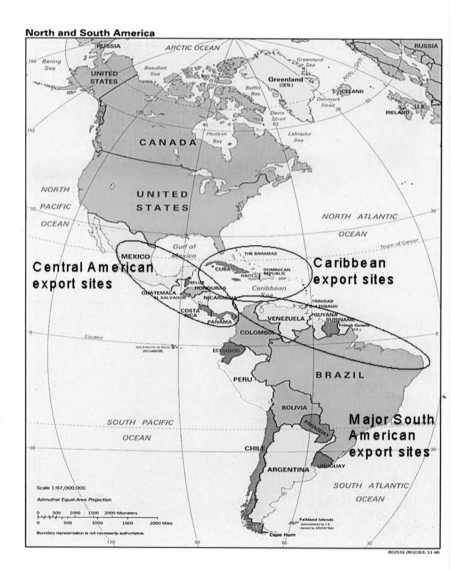

Regions where many enslaved Africans were first shipped during the seventeenth and eighteenth centuries (from The Skeletal Biology of the New York African Burial Ground, Part 1*).*

Divining the cause of death, an African funeral rite practiced in Jamaica, a Caribbean island (from Phillipo 1843) (from Historical Perspectives of the African Burial Ground).

Arrival in Manhattan

Enslaved Africans typically arrived in New York sick from abuse, hunger, dehydration, and diseases carried on board overcrowded ships. On dry land, they were stripped naked, examined like livestock, and auctioned off to the highest bidder. Although they arrived in New York with almost no clothes or personal belongings, they brought with them something no one could take away: their African heritage. They brought their beliefs, customs, and traditions from their homelands. They used their knowledge and skills to create a new life on the island of Manhattan. The New York colonists stole their labor, but they could not erase their memories, crush their spirits, or rob them of their humanity.

The African Community

Euroamerican enslavers saw Africans as chattel, or property, and thus they often gave them new names to suit their own tastes. The enslaved kept their true names and identities in their minds and histories and used them only among themselves or in secret when performing traditional rituals from their homelands. New York's closely knit African community, a mix of the free and enslaved, grew quietly. Early on, some owned land and prospered, and they helped other enslaved Africans when they could. They gathered together in homes, on the streets, and in taverns. They held large, hidden gatherings in the countryside, where Africans from different cultures would dance, sing, and share stories and information. Sometimes, hundreds would join these gatherings and celebrate their distinct heritages. They were nonetheless a people united by common ethnic ties, common interests, marriage, and children. They stitched together the fabrics of their combined African backgrounds to form a new African life in New York.

The Market House (or Meal Market), where Africans were bought, sold, and hired (from Bruce 1898) (from Historical Perspectives of the African Burial Ground).

Festivals

In many British colonies, large numbers of Euroamericans and enslaved Africans participated in rural festivals at which different African groups shared dances, music, and other revelries. In colonial New York, enslaved Africans gathered without threat of punishment during Pinkster parades in honor of the Dutch holiday of Pentecost, the Irish St. Patrick's Day, New Year's Day, and celebrations of the English monarch's coronation and birthday. Many of these festivals took on a decidedly African character, with vibrant singing, dancing, and drumming. Such festivals and other gatherings were an opportunity for enslaved Africans to strengthen their own ethnic identities and in some cases, resist the imposition of their enslavers' identities upon them.

An early depiction of Africans and Europeans dancing at the market, probably produced in the late-eighteenth or early-nineteenth century. This image appeared originally in Our Firemen: A History of the New York Fire Departments, Volunteer and Paid, from 1609 to 1887, *by Augustine Costello (from* Historical Perspectives of the African Burial Ground).

DAILY LIFE

CHAPTER 5

For enslaved Africans, life in Manhattan was different from life in Africa or the Caribbean in many ways. In the Caribbean, Africans had lived together with other Africans in their own spaces. In Manhattan, far away from loved ones, enslaved Africans faced an unfamiliar city, unknown languages, and foods and smells that were foreign to them. They had no choice but to live in households with their enslavers' families, servants, and other enslaved Africans. They usually had to sleep in detached houses that also served as kitchens or in cramped cellars and attics. Their discomforts were many: enslaved Africans had to perform hard labor, were given little to eat, and had to endure cold winters with few garments. Many were poorly clothed, and new arrivals sometimes had to find or steal cloth, thread, and buttons to make their own clothes. Disease and violence were rampant among the enslaved African population. The skeletons of numerous individuals buried at the New York African Burial Ground show signs of physical injury suffered during their lifetimes. Many died at young ages.

City Life

The colonial city of New York was a very different place from the early Dutch settlement of the 1600s. By the early 1700s, the small community in Lower Manhattan with a few hundred residents had become a bustling city of several thousand people. New York expanded steadily northward and westward, creating demand for ever more African labor. By 1741, New York City was around a mile long and a little over half a mile wide. It had a population of about 10,000 people, of whom nearly 2,000 were Africans.

New York City was also a mixture of different cultures, languages, and religions. It was a busy place, with seven wards or sections. The Dock, South, and East Wards along the East River waterfront were dense with people. The Bowery and Haarlem (modern-day Harlem) Wards to the northeast contained rolling farmland. Most New Yorkers were merchants, shopkeepers, or traders.

Clothing

Colonial New York City's enslaved Africans did not always have adequate clothing to protect themselves from the elements. They wore the typical clothes of the day: breeches, a shirt, jacket, and cap for men; and for women, a skirt, petticoat, blouse, and hat. Shoes may have been worn mostly during the winter months. Many of these items were not provided by enslavers, and as a result, enslaved women quickly became experienced in making European-style clothing, and there were many African tailors in the city. Many enslaved Africans had to resort to stealing cloth, buttons, and thread to expand their wardrobe. For instance, 18-year-old Hannah was punished for stealing materials to make a gown, petticoat, and handkerchief. She took that risk because she had almost no clothing to wear.

Much of what is known of the clothing of enslaved Africans comes from advertisements about escapees. These notices provided many details about the escaped person's wardrobe, appearance, skills, and language use. For instance, an African named Tom escaped in the fall of 1777 wearing trousers, a checked shirt, and a striped jacket fastened with pieces of fabric tape, but no shoes or stockings. Lucretia escaped with a larger wardrobe. In the winter of 1763, she took with her a black petticoat, a white apron, a speckled handkerchief, a blue waistcoat, a laced cap, and a blue cloak.

Men's everyday breeches: from left to right, *linen cotton (1765–1785), cotton velvet (1785–1825), and yellow "nankeen" cotton (1785–1815)*. Colonial Williamsburg Collection (The Colonial Williamsburg Foundation).

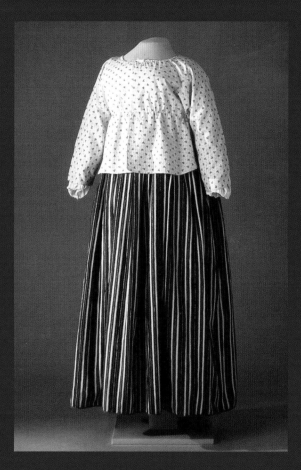

Quilted petticoat (1770–1775). Colonial Williamsburg Collection (The Colonial Williamsburg Foundation).

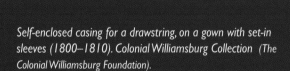

Self-enclosed casing for a drawstring, on a gown with set-in sleeves (1800–1810). Colonial Williamsburg Collection (The Colonial Williamsburg Foundation).

Working woman's striped linen wool petticoat (1770–1820), topped by a high-waisted short gown made from cotton linen (1800–1820). Colonial Williamsburg Collection (The Colonial Williamsburg Foundation).

All images on this page are from The Archaeology of the New York African Burial Ground, *Part 1*.

Major streets were filled with pedestrians, carriages, and carts loaded with merchandise. Piers and streets echoed with the sound of rolling barrels being pushed over cobblestones. During the summer, the port was a forest of masts, and sailors mingled with farmers going to market. Ever-watchful soldiers in red coats carried long muskets. Throughout the city, Africans carried heavy loads on their heads and weaved through the crowds. They carried baskets of fish, sides of beef, bundles of clothing, or lumber. The entire life of the city depended on enslaved African labor.

Work in Colonial New York City

The work assigned to enslaved New York Africans also was different from work on Caribbean plantations or in Africa. Early on, many enslaved Africans in Manhattan worked on farms or in building the settlement. As the city grew, it bustled with activity. It was a port city, where products from the region were sent to be sold to other colonies. Of the many jobs to be done in New York, enslaved Africans did almost every type, from skilled work to hard labor.

Most of New York's enslaved Africans were laborers who worked along the waterfront or on the land. Enslaved men also drove carts filled with merchandise between the docks and merchant warehouses. About 40 percent of the sailors on British merchant ships were African, and many piloted small boats that crisscrossed the harbor. African teams loaded and unloaded huge, heavy barrels on ships, a backbreaking and dangerous task.

Skilled manufacturing jobs were also done by enslaved Africans in New York. They worked alongside their enslavers and other workers, although laws limited their use in skilled jobs. They worked in industries such as metalworking, flour milling, snuff making, and beer brewing. They labored in workshops that housed shipbuilders and wheelwrights, blacksmiths and barrel makers. Shipbuilding was a skilled and labor-intensive task to which many enslaved African New Yorkers were assigned. Even a simple vessel required months of skilled carpentry and the use of a broad range of tools. Africans carried the timbers and planking used in shipbuilding on their shoulders and made many a ship's rigging and cordage. They also made barrels for ships and warehouses, a craft that required advanced woodworking skills. African coopers made barrels so well that some Euroamerican colonists petitioned the New York Assembly in 1743 to keep Africans from working in the industry. Their petition met with little success, however.

Skilled Labor

Enslaved Africans performed a wide and impressive range of tasks in colonial New York City. For instance, when tailor John Dunn died in 1730, his widow Mary offered for sale "two very good Negro Men Slaves Taylors, and one Negro Man Slave, a Butcher and Sawyer." Sailmaker Francis Vincent, who died 3 years later, left "two young Negro Men, both good Sail-Makers." These enslaved Africans probably were sold quickly and for high prices, as the demand for enslaved people with special skills was great.

Many merchants entrusted enslaved Africans to work in their small shops. Enslaved Africans also worked for lawyers and doctors, as well as artisans of all types. Although enslaved Africans were not paid for their labor, they were aware of the value of their skills. When Saxton, an enslaved carpenter and cooper for Jacobus Cortlandt, ran away in 1733, the notice of his escape stated that he took his "Tools for Both Trades" with him.

Ropewalk, a colonial industry where enslaved laborers worked (from Bridenbaugh 1950) (from Historical Perspectives of the African Burial Ground).

The Townsend MacCoun Map, showing the many wharves and ship yards where African New Yorkers worked (courtesy the New York Public Library Map Division) (from Historical Perspectives of the African Burial Ground).

Enslaved Africans were often assigned to the most unpleasant jobs. Many African men worked in slaughterhouses and tanneries or cleaned up filth in the streets. Some industries that produced toxic fumes were located on the outskirts of the city, near the site of the African Burial Ground. These industries polluted the environment and dumped their trash in the burial ground. Many enslaved African men performed duties that were considered "heavy craft," such as transporting and drying large animal hides. After soaking the hides in lye to remove hair from the skins, the Africans had to rub and soften them using bear's oil so the leather could be made into shoes, harnesses, and other goods.

Difficult and varied types of women's labor was performed by African women mostly in enslavers' homes. Working from before dawn and into the night, enslaved African women cooked and preserved food, looked after children, cleaned houses, and did laundry. Endless tasks filled their days: brewing alcohol, sewing, spinning, weaving, carrying water, and cooking meals in a detached "Negro kitchen." As cooks, they wrestled every day with heavy pots, and constant lifting was an everyday burden.

Children as young as 6–12 years old were also forced to work. The very young assisted in domestic work or helped to serve meals. Some were taught skilled trades at an early age, as children were thought to be easier to control.

The Effects of Work

The New York African Burial Ground researchers studied the remains of the people buried at the project site to learn how repetitive tasks and hard labor affected the bodies of the deceased. They examined bones and joints for stress-related damage and for signs of injury from possible work-related accidents. Places on the skeletons where muscles attached to bones were also studied to determine what repeated motions stressed and damaged the skeletons. For example, enslaved Africans were constantly climbing stairs, ropewalks, and ladders to perform many difficult tasks. They carried very heavy loads, often on their heads, over uneven ground. Such work day after day, year after year, frequently led to joint problems in their legs, arms, lower backs, and necks. The researchers found signs of physical stress from work in the bones of children as young as 4 years old. In some individuals, stress was indicated by bone hypertrophy, or an unusually large increase in bone density and thickness.

Ankle problems were common among the people buried at the burial ground. Lifting and carrying heavy loads injured the spine and elbows of many, particularly those of men. Women suffered from strain caused by repeated back-and-forth motions

Typical kitchen in a colonial household where Africans lived and worked.

Musculoskeletal Stress Markers

Archaeologists can learn about the kinds of work people did by studying those places on a skeleton where muscle attachments are overdeveloped or damaged. The exact activity that affected the skeleton cannot be known, but these stress markers show which muscle groups and bones were heavily affected by work. Historical information can then be used to learn what kinds of work may have caused stress. Stress markers, which result from repeated physical activity over long periods, can also be used to learn about the severity of work-related stress. For instance, a male aged 35–50 (Burial 97) had stress markers on over half of his muscle attachments. This man may have been forced to do extremely heavy labor over a long period of enslavement. For a male aged 15–24 (Burial 323), moderate to severe stress markers were seen on more than a third of his attachments. Given his age, this man may have been forced into heavy labor while young.

Burials 369, 174, and 223 (see images at right) showed evidence of hypertrophy, or thickening of the bone, indicative of repetitive motion. Overall, the large number of stress markers found in the sample suggest that heavy lifting was common for the enslaved Africans buried at the project site. Stress markers were frequent in both males and females. The greater occurrence in males suggests that enslaved males were more often forced into heavy labor or labor that affected more places on the skeleton than were enslaved women.

All images on this page are from The Skeletal Biology of the New York African Burial Ground, *Part 1*.

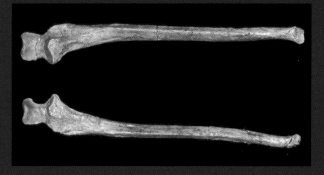

Severe hypertrophy in a male aged 40–50 years (Burial 369).

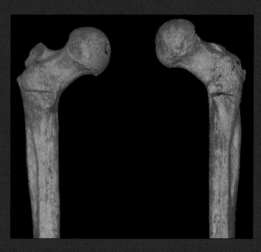

Hypertrophy in a male aged 17–18 years (Burial 174).

Hypertrophy in a female aged 25–35 years (Burial 223).

of the arms, typical of people who grind grain or wash clothes. Often their hands and wrists were injured, probably from spinning thread, weaving, and other manual jobs. Broken bones and dislocated joints were additional results of their hard labor. Dislocations cannot always be determined by examining the skeleton alone, and they probably happened much more often than the burial ground researchers reported. Overall, the harsh effects of hard work on the bodies of enslaved Africans lowered their quality of life and quite possibly led to other health problems.

Diet

By studying historical information and bones and teeth, the New York African Burial Ground researchers learned about the foods enslaved African New Yorkers ate and their effects on health. The skeletons of the individuals buried at the site tell a tale of poor diet and hunger. Historical records showed that the diets of enslaved Africans in New York were based on maize, or corn. Mostly, the enslaved ate porridges made with maize, and sometimes those porridges were also made with milk, salted meat, or vegetables. Fresh meat was rare, however, and fruits and vegetables were eaten only when they were in season. When possible, enslaved Africans stole or traded for better food. They also hunted wild game, caught fish, and collected wild plants. They ate oysters, which were and are common in New York, when they were available.

Maize is not always a very nutritious food. Depending on how it is prepared, eating a diet based on maize can lead to malnutrition. Malnutrition, along with unsanitary living conditions, can cause porotic hyperostosis, a condition seen often in the bones of the persons buried at the African Burial Ground. The outer surface of bone afflicted with this condition appears pitted and spongy. A lack of Vitamin B12, which can be found in meat and fish, is one potential cause of pitted and spongy bones. A similar bone condition that occurs around the eye sockets—cribra orbitalia—can result from similar causes, which may also include a lack of Vitamin C in diets. More than half of the 275 people examined for pitted and spongy bones at the New York African Burial Ground showed evidence of this condition, indicating that many enslaved Africans could have suffered from a poor diet.

Porotic hyperostosis can also result from infectious disease. Unsanitary living conditions could lead to infection, which causes further loss of important nutrients. Nutrient loss caused by parasites was common in enslaved African communities in the Caribbean and may also have been a health risk in colonial New York.

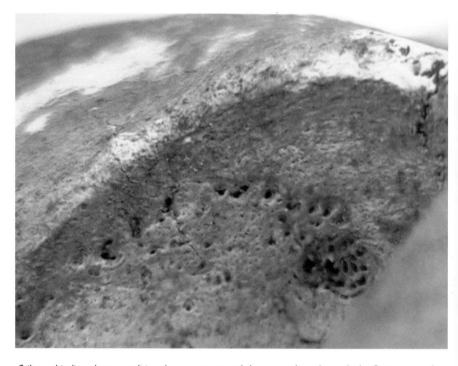

Cribra orbitalia, a bone condition that occurs around the eye sockets due to lack of vitamins in the diet, can be seen in the pitted surface of the eye socket above (Burial 6, 25–30-year-old male) (from The Skeletal Biology of the New York African Burial Ground, Part 1).

Skeletal Evidence of Malnutrition

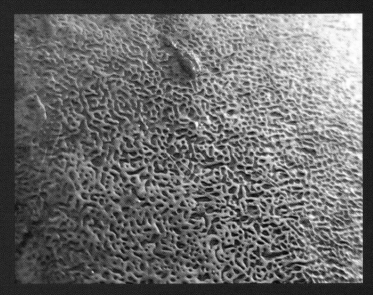

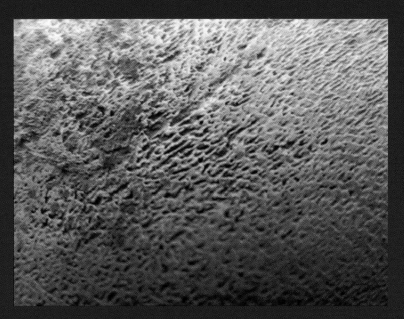

Evidence of porotic hyperostosis, a sign of malnutrition in which the surface of bones appears pitted and spongy, in the bones of a 3–5-year-old child (Burial 138) (from The Skeletal Biology of the New York African Burial Ground, Part 1).

Porotic hyperostosis in a 4.5–10.5-month-old child (Burial 64) (from The Skeletal Biology of the New York African Burial Ground, Part 1).

Thickening of the diploe, the spongy tissue between the inside and outside layer of the skull, in a 35–45-year-old male (Burial 151) compared with a normal specimen (from The Skeletal Biology of the New York African Burial Ground, Part 1).

Cribra orbitalia of the right socket of a 5–7-year-old child (Burial 39) (from The Skeletal Biology of the New York African Burial Ground, Part 1).

Roundworms, pork tapeworms, Guinea worms, and hookworms breed freely in houses with damp, dirt floors and poor sanitation. Enslaved Africans in the Americas sometimes ate earth because their bodies were starved for nutrients, which also could have been a cause of worm infection.

Genetics and environment also may have contributed to the widespread malnutrition among the enslaved Africans. People throughout the world, including many Africans, have a genetic characteristic that prevents them from digesting milk or cheese properly. They experience pain if they eat these foods, which are rich in calcium and protein. Genetics may also have contributed to the lack of Vitamin D, which is produced in the body from the sun's rays on the skin. In New York's northern climate, dark skin may have prevented Vitamin D production in Africans. All of these problems—poor diets, unsanitary living conditions, inability to digest cheese or milk, and a lack of Vitamin D—would have led to malnutrition in New York's enslaved Africans.

Additionally, the simple act of eating may have been a problem for enslaved Africans because of the condition of their teeth. Diet and poor dental care cause tooth loss, caries (cavities), and abscessed (infected) teeth. Researchers noted caries on many of the teeth unearthed at the New York African Burial Ground. Diets rich in carbohydrates, like those based on maize, and a lack of dental hygiene may have helped caries to form. Dental abscesses are infections of the mouth, face, jaw, or throat caused by cavities or infected teeth. Abscesses for the burial ground sample were high compared to those for other groups of the same period. If they spread too far, dental abscesses can cause death. Tooth loss was also common among the burial ground sample. Men and women in the sample had an average of four missing teeth. Those teeth could have been lost from caries, dental abscesses, or accidents. Chewing food would have been difficult for many enslaved African New Yorkers, given the scope of dental problems seen in the individuals buried at the project site.

Another problem was lead poisoning, common among Euroamerican elites of the time who ate off pewter dishes made with lead. It was also common in the Caribbean, where the locally distilled rum was often tainted with lead. The burial ground researchers were surprised to find extremely high levels of lead in some of the bones sampled. They found that Africans who spent a long time in New York had the highest lead levels, whereas those born in Africa had low lead levels. Irritability, low appetite, low energy, hearing loss, headaches, slowed body growth, anemia, constipation, and kidney damage are among the effects of lead poisoning. Lead poisoning would have caused major health problems for enslaved Africans, especially children.

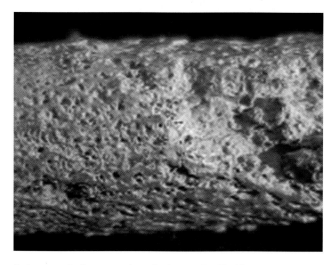

Indicators of infection on the right femur of a 50–60-year-old male (Burial 32) (from The Skeletal Biology of the New York African Burial Ground, *Part 1).*

Indicators of infection on the right femur of a 50–60-year-old male (Burial 32), magnified (from The Skeletal Biology of the New York African Burial Ground, *Part 1).*

Variations in Lead Levels and Potential Lead Poisoning

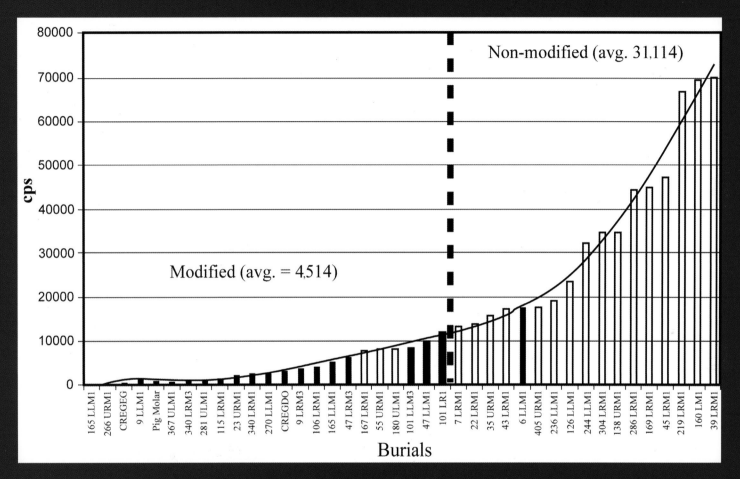

The New York African Burial Ground researchers were surprised to find extremely high levels of lead in some of the bones and teeth sampled, suggesting that lead poisoning was a serious health problem for enslaved Africans. As this chart reveals, much lower levels of lead were found in the teeth of Africans who had modified teeth and may have been born in Africa (black bars) compared to those who may have been born in New York (white bars) (from The Skeletal Biology of the New York African Burial Ground, Part 1).

The source of lead poisoning is not yet known, but contaminated food containers or alcohol are possible sources. Problems with digestion and eating, poor diets, and lead poisoning may have served to weaken the enslaved Africans of New York, who were already suffering from the negative effects of forced, hard labor.

Infectious Disease

Cities were unhealthy places during the eighteenth century, and outbreaks of disease in urban areas were common. In New York City, poor sanitation, contaminated water, and crowded dwellings all contributed to the spread of disease. Smallpox outbreaks occurred there at least four times during the 1700s. Many of New York City's enslaved Africans had survived the disease in their youth, due to an African tradition of inoculating the healthy. Other common diseases included yellow fever, malaria, typhoid, whooping cough, diphtheria, and influenza. A yellow fever epidemic in 1702 killed hundreds of New York City residents in just a few months, nearly 10 percent of the population. New York African Burial Ground researchers identified yaws or, alternatively, congenital syphilis, which is acquired in the womb, in 40 of the people buried at the New York African Burial Ground. Congenital syphilis may have been acquired by their mothers in the Caribbean, where syphilis was common, and passed on to them as babies before birth.

Often caused by infectious disease, periostitis is the abnormal growth of bone tissue seen in the outer membrane of a bone. Almost two-thirds of the people buried in the New York African Burial Ground had periostitis, indicating they had at least one serious infection and were affected by unknown diseases. For children, infections were often lethal, while adults more often survived the infection.

Stress

Another sign of malnutrition, disease, or severe stress is dental enamel hypoplasias. These are grooves or pits on teeth where enamel stopped growing during a period of childhood stress. No less than 70 percent of a sample of the individuals with permanent dentition buried at the site had hypoplasias. Hypoplasias were most common for the children in this sample who died before age 15, as more than 86 percent had the condition. The numbers fall to 76.5 percent for the enslaved Africans between 15 and 24 years of age. Around two-thirds of those who died at ages over 24 had the condition. Fewer than half of those who died at an old age had hypoplasias.

Indicators of infection on a 35–45-year-old male, magnified (Burial 70) *(from* The Skeletal Biology of the New York African Burial Ground, Part 1*)*.

Indicators of infection on an adult male (Burial 69) *(from* The Skeletal Biology of the New York African Burial Ground, Part 1*)*.

Malnutrition and Stress: Dental Evidence

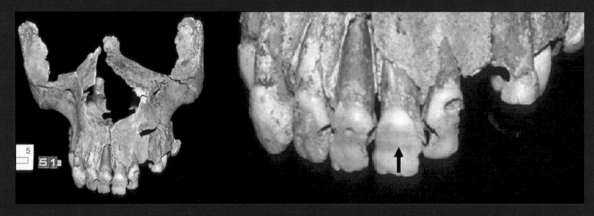

Left, *bands of discoloration caused by hypocalcification in a 24–32-year-old female (Burial 51);* right, *magnification (from* The Skeletal Biology of the New York African Burial Ground, *Part 1).*

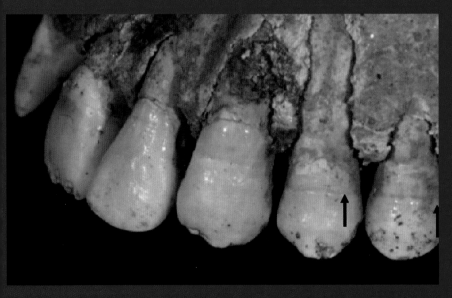

Linear enamel hypoplastic lesions in teeth of a female ag ed 20–25 years (Burial 1) (from The Skeletal Biology of the New York African Burial Ground, *Part 1).*

Deciduous mandibular dentition with a single non-linear hypoplastic pit in the right canine of a subadult aged 3–5 years (Burial 7). This individual also appears to have been anemic (from The Skeletal Biology of the New York African Burial Ground, *Part 1).*

These numbers suggest that Africans who grew up enslaved as children had much more childhood stress than those who were enslaved as adults. Malnutrition would have been part of this stress.

The study of hypoplasias suggests that many children of enslaved Africans were stressed between the ages of 3½ and 6. The historical evidence shows that enslaved children in New York were often sold at a young age. Separated from their parents and placed in unfamiliar households, they were given poor diets, exposed to different diseases, and forced to work. By the age of 14, enslaved African children were considered adults, which would have increased the stresses on those children pressed into hard labor. Hypoplasias that were found in children in the sample between the ages of 9 and 16 also correspond to historical records of importations of large numbers of African children of these ages into New York. Hypoplasias provide additional physical evidence that the Middle Passage and the harsh quality of life for enslaved Africans in New York were highly stressful and life threatening for them and their children.

Families and Children

Project researchers observed a pattern of little or no population growth among the enslaved Africans in colonial New York. Their review of the biological data suggests that African New Yorkers died at young ages; also, many were chronically unhealthy, which would have reduced birth rates. Their review of historical census data revealed a low ratio of children to adult females among enslaved Africans. For a population to grow, a ratio of 2 to 1, or at least 2 children per adult female, is needed. In most years in early New York City, not enough African children were born to replace the number of Africans who died. Occasional higher ratios of children to women can be traced to large numbers of children imported into New York, however, not to child-bearing. Yet these children, as well as children born to African parents in New York, also died at a high rate and did not survive to have children themselves. As a result, the city's African population grew slowly, despite constant new arrivals.

Historical research suggests that enslaved Africans were discouraged from having families, and when they did, the children were often separated from the parents and deprived of the care they needed to survive. Sustaining a family was made very difficult for enslaved Africans, who often were prevented from seeing loved ones or raising their

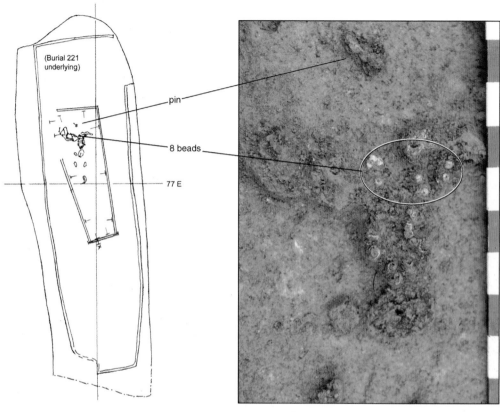

The photograph on the right shows the scant remains of the infant in Burial 226 with eight fired-glass beads worn at the neck. Interred in its own coffin, the infant was found within the grave of Burial 221, a man between the ages of 30 and 60 (shown in drawing at left) (drawing by M. Schur; photograph by Dennis Seckler) (from The Archaeology of the New York African Burial Ground, Part 1).

Mementos

Findings at the New York African Burial Ground suggest that, in some instances, meaningful objects were buried with children. Perhaps these keepsakes were given to them by loving family members, or they could have been precious offerings intended to accompany the children into the next world. The 1.5–4-year-old child in Burial 187 was buried with 22 black beads. Drawn and cut from glass made in Europe, the beads were wrapped around the child's hips. Eight yellow beads were discovered near the jaw of the infant in Burial 226. These beads are similar to those produced in what is now southern Ghana. A glass-and-wire ornament was found on the cranium of an infant less than 2 months old (Burial 186). In another instance, a pear-shaped silver pendant was found with the 3.5–5.5-year-old child in Burial 254. Found near the jaw, it may have been worn as an earring or on a cord around the neck. The meaning of these items will never be known, but they could have served as eternal links to family members, origins, or traditions.

All images on this page are from The Archaeology of the New York African Burial Ground, *Part 1.*

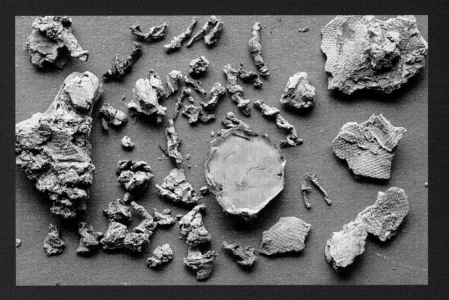

Copper-alloy and glass jewelry/ornament from Burial 186 (photograph by Jon Abbott).

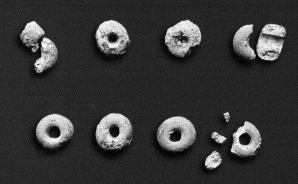

Donut-shaped opaque yellow beads from Burial 226 (photograph by Jon Abbott).

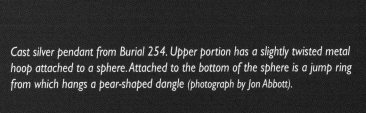

Cast silver pendant from Burial 254. Upper portion has a slightly twisted metal hoop attached to a sphere. Attached to the bottom of the sphere is a jump ring from which hangs a pear-shaped dangle (photograph by Jon Abbott).

own children. When they did have families, the prospect of sale or separation was always looming. Few enslavers tried to keep families together when they bought or sold enslaved Africans. These forced separations and the constant cleaving of families would have been one more hardship to endure for enslaved Africans in New York, who had already been separated from loved ones in Africa. Yet evidence for shared graves, grave groupings, and other findings at the New York African Burial Ground suggest that the individuals buried there succeeded in creating and preserving some family ties.

As noted, growth among the enslaved African population in New York City came mostly from imports. The harsh quality of life and chronic disease and stress seen in biological data likely prevented enslaved women from having children at normal rates, and African couples had few children on average. In addition to enduring harsh labor conditions, enslaved African mothers were poorly nourished and often suffered from chronic infections. Their enslavers were sometimes cruel and unforgiving toward African babies and their mothers. Fertility and infant care were discouraged, and unions between men and women were often disrupted to prevent pregnancy. Caring for pregnant women or infants increased the costs of their upkeep and decreased the amount of work enslavers expected enslaved women to do. Childbirth could also result in the death of the mother, which would have meant a total loss of an enslaver's investment. A steady flow of work and profit and the decrease in costs would have been most important to enslavers, and few showed concern for the health and welfare of enslaved Africans and their children. The large number of infants buried at the New York African Burial Ground reflects the high risk of childbearing and the hardships women and infants endured.

Death

The project researchers used skeletal data to learn about mortality rates for the African population in colonial New York City. Euroamerican deaths were recorded in Trinity Church's death records. African deaths were not recorded, so the ages at which Africans died could only be learned from studying the bones of the people buried at the project site. Historical data indicate that childbirth for women and violence among young men claimed the lives of many Euroamerican individuals of the period. Both Euroamericans and Africans tended to die at young ages, but many Euroamericans lived longer due to better nutrition, living conditions, and quality of life.

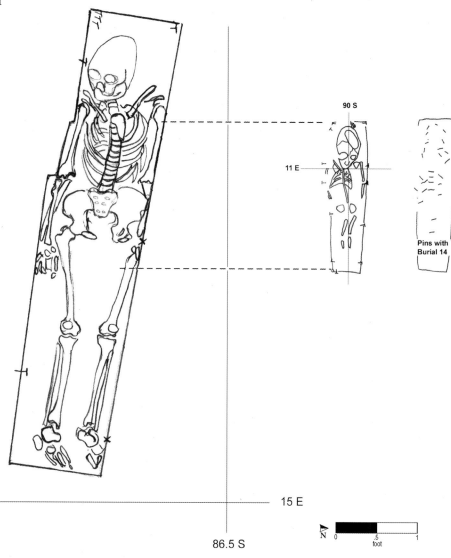

Burial 14 contained an infant no more than 6 months old who shared a grave with a 35–45-year-old woman (Burial 12). The child's coffin was placed inside the woman's coffin. At right is an excavator's drawing of pins that encircled the infant's skull (at top) and extended down to the knees (from The Archaeology of the New York African Burial Ground, Part 2*).*

Mother and Child Shared Graves

Infants were sometimes buried with adults in a shared grave; in the case of Burial 335, a 25–35-year-old woman was buried with an infant (Burial 356) under her arm. In Burial 12, the tiny coffin of an infant (Burial 14) was tucked into the coffin of a 35–45-year-old woman. Because the woman and child were buried at the same time, we can infer a mother and child relationship; perhaps the woman died in childbirth or both were taken by the same illness. An intriguing grouping consisted of two small coffins, which held a child 6–12 months of age (Burial 144) and an infant/newborn (Burial 149), resting on the coffin of a 25–30-year-old woman (Burial 142). Project researchers concluded that the three could have been buried at the same time, or that the children could have been placed in the woman's grave at a later time. Although it cannot be assumed that the woman was the mother of one or either of the children, this shared burial clearly suggests a close relationship among the three in life.

A woman and two children in a shared grave (Burials 142, 144, and 149). The outlines of the individual coffins are indicated (photograph by Dennis Seckler) (from The Archaeology of the New York African Burial Ground, *Part 1).*

Using statistical analysis, the researchers studied the demographics of the New York African Burial Ground population. Demography is the study of population structure according to variables like age, sex, ethnicity, and occupation. Their studies showed that the enslaved Africans died at younger ages than did their Euroamerican peers and that many of the African dead were children. For all the people recovered from the burial ground, the average age at death was 22.3 years. Nearly 45 percent died at ages under 15, and more than half of the children buried at the site died by the age of 2. Many of the adults died in their twenties or thirties. Eighty percent of the women died by age 40. Men more often survived to older ages, but few enslaved Africans survived to old age. Enslaved African women in particular died at an age when they were capable of having children.

Mortality statistics from the burial ground sample reflect the percentage of men, women, and children in New York's African population. The Trinity Church records show that many European men died between the ages of 25 and 30. This probably reflects both large numbers of young men and the dangerous lifestyles they led. Generally, large numbers of children in a burial population can occur when there are many more children than adults in the population. Without census data for African births and deaths, it is hard to say whether the large number of children in the New York African Burial Ground site reflects a population at risk, a large population of children, or both.

In either case, African New Yorkers experienced a poor quality of life with respect to other groups who lived in the area. Euroamericans were five times more likely than Africans to survive past the age of 55. The high mortality for the enslaved Africans can almost certainly be linked to the harsh effects of their enslavement, which included hard labor, poor nutrition, violence, and disease.

Adult Mortality: New York African Burial Ground and Trinity Church

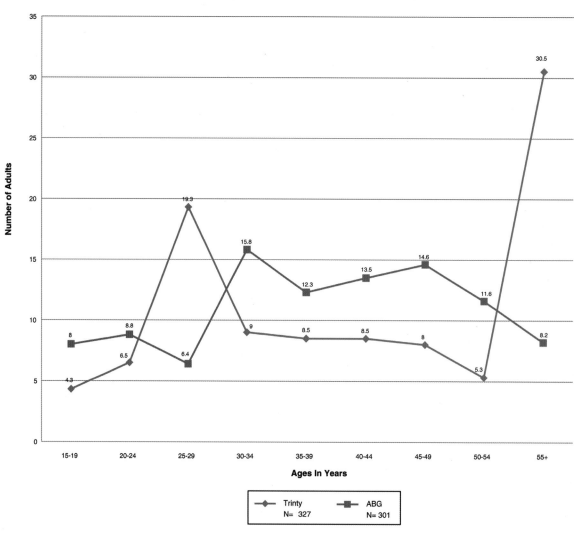

As this chart shows, the New York African Burial Ground researchers found substantial differences between the mortality rates (years of life) of the individuals buried at their study site, who were overwhelmingly of African descent (red bar), and those buried during the same time period in New York City's Trinity Church Cemetery, who were predominantly of European origin (blue bar) (from The Skeletal Biology of the New York African Burial Ground, Part I).

Skeletal Age and Sex Distributions

New York African Burial Ground researchers studied age-at-death for males, females, and children buried at the site. They calculated age-at-death using known characteristics of bones and teeth that correspond to different ages. Sex could only be determined accurately for the mature individuals, so the sex of children and infants could not be learned from the skeleton(s). Studying age and sex distributions allowed the researchers to determine the ages at which the buried children and adult men and women had died. Clearly, many young African children and infants in New York died before their second year. Also, males and females among the enslaved tended to die at different ages. This pattern could correspond to different health hazards, such as childbirth, or major differences in the typical ages of African men and women living in New York City.

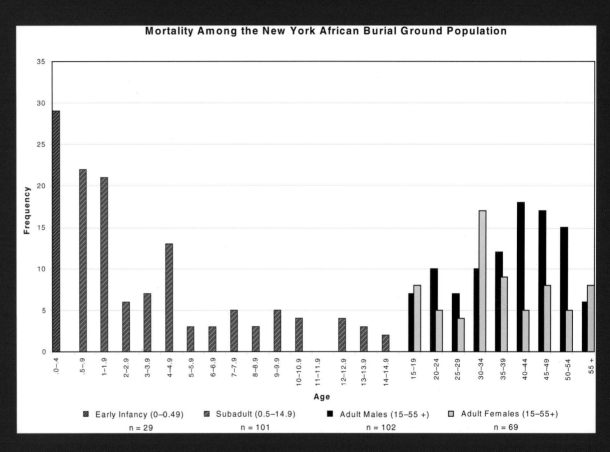

Bar graph representing sex and age at death using average ages for the 301 individuals observable for age and/or sex. More than half the children at the burial ground died by the age of two, and many adults died in their twenties and thirties (from The Skeletal Biology of the New York African Burial Ground, *Part 1).*

A Sacred Place

Used by thousands of people of African descent for more than a century, the African Burial Ground became a sacred place. There, New York Africans could more openly practice traditional rituals from their homelands and act on their spiritual beliefs. Funerals were a focal point of their community life, and through burial ritual, enslaved Africans and their descendants communed with their ancestors and strengthened their ties to African heritages in ways their daily lives did not allow. In addition to showing respect for the deceased, burial rituals also reinforced the Africans' beliefs about death and the afterlife. Such beliefs were a powerful source of guidance and strength for the New York African community.

Historical accounts suggest that African New Yorkers buried their own dead at the burial ground. Although little is known of the rituals they performed at the graveside, those rituals were very likely different from those of the European Christians who enslaved them. Some Christian practices may have been used, but they were probably interpreted in terms of African beliefs and practices. African dance, drumming, and song were probably common at funerals. In all likelihood, the New York Africans' funerals shared some similarities with funerals in their homelands and drew upon diverse African traditions. They were an opportunity for people of African descent to find common ground and strengthen community ties.

A Standard Way to Bury the Dead

Although only a portion of the burial ground was excavated, the New York African Burial Ground researchers found that the burials that were excavated there were remarkably similar. Nearly everyone was buried lying on his or her back with his or her body fully extended. Only one individual may have been buried on his side. No person was buried face down, in a sitting position, or with their knees bent, as if in a fetal position.

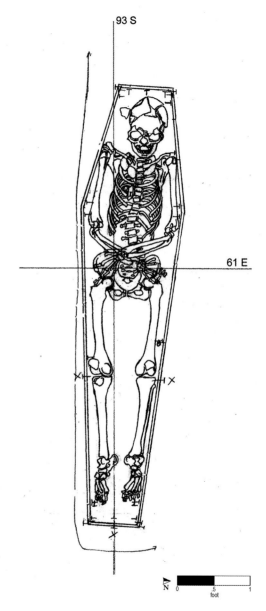

Burial of an 18–20-year-old female in extended supine position with hands crossed over pelvic region (Burial 122) (drawing by M. Schur) (from The Archaeology of the New York African Burial Ground, *Part 2).*

Interment in the African Burial Ground would have been carried out by members of the African community (illustration by Michael Colbert, 2004) (from Historical Perspectives of the African Burial Ground).

In only one case, an individual was clearly removed illegally, dissected, and replaced with the bones out of anatomical order.

Nearly all the persons buried in the recovered burials were buried with their heads pointing to the west, toward the setting sun. Most were placed in individual coffins, even in shared graves. Research suggests that those buried without coffins in the burial ground may have died during the Revolutionary War. Those burials may have lacked coffins because the deceased had no friends or family around to tend to a more fitting burial. Because enslaved Africans lived in extreme poverty, few people were buried with personal possessions. Many were buried in shrouds or in their street clothes.

The project researchers did not expect to find such similar treatment of nearly all the burials, but that was indeed the case. They expected that the diverse origins of the African New Yorkers would have led to different burial practices. Could the excavated area contain only people from a specific area in Africa or from a particular religious group? This seems unlikely, for the excavated area was in constant use over a long period. Enslaved Africans from many groups arrived in New York City over many generations, both from the Caribbean and directly from West Africa. It seems unlikely that the excavated burials reflect only one group, nor were any religious symbols, such as crucifixes, discovered to point consistently to one predominant form of belief.

Could it be that the Euroamerican authorities governed the disposal of the corpses so strictly or that sextons made sure that burials were conducted in the same way? This seems unlikely, because as far as could be determined, no one ever managed the burial ground. Also, the few available historical descriptions suggest that the Africans themselves controlled their burial ceremonies. Enslavers may have been required to provide coffins for the burial of deceased enslaved Africans, however. Between 1753 and 1756, for example, the cabinetmaker Joseph Delaplaine filled orders for 13 coffins that were used to bury deceased Africans, but no records could be found to show that coffins were required. A requirement to use coffins could explain why nearly all Africans were placed on their backs with their bodies fully extended—to fit inside a typical coffin. But this would not explain why the African dead were always oriented in the same way in the grave or other aspects of burial discovered there.

One possibility is that the enslaved Africans decided early on how to bury their dead. This could mean that the African community in New York was close-knit from the very beginning.

The Doctors' Riot

In the late 1700s, medical doctors stole corpses from graves in New York City to study anatomy and conduct medical experiments. Several cemeteries were robbed, including the African Burial Ground, the almshouse cemetery on the Commons, and a private cemetery on Gold Street. In one case, the records reveal, "The Corpse of a Young gentleman from the West Indias, was ... taken up—the grave left open, & the funeral clothing scatterd about" (April 16, 1788 letter from Colonel William Heth to Edmund Randolph, Governor of Virginia). The outraged public rioted in April 1788 to protest this desecration.

One burial in the New York African Burial Ground showed possible evidence of grave robbing. A 25–35-year-old man (Burial 364) was buried without a coffin, and his remains were placed in a puzzling fashion. Some skeletal elements were placed in correct anatomical position, but others were not. For instance, the right forearm bones were placed where the lower left leg should have been. Cut marks on bones showed that the hands and lower arms had been severed near the time of death. One interpretation of these remains is that this body had been stolen from the burial ground, partially dissected, and reburied. Alternatively, if dismemberment occurred prior to or near the time of death, this individual could have been the victim of a brutal and torturous execution.

Another individual's burial (Burial 323) suggests that his grave too might have been disturbed. That man, aged 19–20 years, held the top of his skull, which had been sawed off, in his arms. At that time, saws were used to cut bone during autopsies or dissection. His strange but tidy reburial remains a mystery.

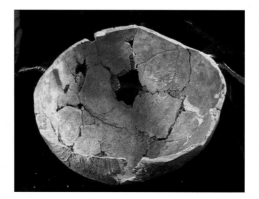

Top of skull from Burial 323 (from The Skeletal Biology of the New York African Burial Ground, Part 1*).*

Magnified saw marks on skull in Burial 323 (from The Skeletal Biology of the New York African Burial Ground, Part 1*).*

84

Burials with Decorative Cuff Links

As the archaeology researchers noted, the expense of even one or two shillings for adornment, such as decorated cufflinks, would have been considerable for most people buried at the African Burial Ground. During the eighteenth century, cuff links were called "sleeve buttons" or "links of buttons" and ranged from very plain to ornate. Only six individuals, three of them coffinless burials, were buried at the New York African Burial Ground with cuff links that the researchers determined were decorative. Some cuff links were missing their shanks, and others were no longer attached to their mates; although these were no longer useful, perhaps they were prized possessions. The 25–35-year-old woman buried without a coffin in Burial 371 was found with two turquoise enamel cuff-link faces under her left upper arm. The distinctive cuff links were decorated with a white-and-pink V and two dots. A probable man in Burial 211, also buried without a coffin, was found with a possible undecorated turquoise enamel cuff-link face near his chin. Researchers noted that he was buried in an apparent north-south row of burials probably dating to after 1776. In another coffinless burial dating to around the same time (Burial 158), a pair of round, gilded copper-alloy cuff links was recovered from each wrist of a 20–30-year-old man. Pairs of octagonal-shaped copper-alloy cuff links with designs impressed into their faces were found with the three men in Burials 238, 341, and 392. The 42–52-year-old man in Burial 392 was buried with two cuff-link faces, one near the spine and another near his right shoulder. He wore clothes when he was buried, as buttons and fibers were also found with his remains. His burial was unusual, as his was one of only four burials with the head oriented to the east identified at the burial ground.

Turquoise enameled cuff link faces on copper-alloy backs, Burial 371. The background is turquoise; the decorative motif is white and pink (photograph by Jon Abbott).

Enamel jewelry/possible cuff-link or button face from Burial 211. The oval face is of turquoise enamel, originally on a copper-alloy backing (photograph by Jon Abbott).

Detail of decorative motif on cuff-link faces from Burial 238.

Two pairs of copper-alloy cuff links were found near the wrists of the 40–50-year-old man in Burial 238, front and back (photograph by Jon Abbott).

Gilt, copper-alloy cuff links from Burial 158 (photograph by Jon Abbott).

Copper-alloy cuff link from Burial 392 (photograph by Jon Abbott).

Despite their many differences, the enslaved Africans may have developed a common African American identity from their shared backgrounds. Future excavations in other areas of the burial ground, should they occur, could reveal whether the practices evident in the excavated section are similar to or different from burials in other areas of the burial ground.

Coffins

More than 90 percent of the graves unearthed at the New York African Burial Ground site contained traces of wooden coffins. All were simple and inexpensive. Most were made of softwoods like cedar, pine, or fir. Three main forms of coffins were used—hexagonal or shouldered caskets, tapered forms, and trapezoidal or rectangular boxes. Some tapered or rectangular coffins had footboards. The more elaborate gable-lidded coffins used for European and Euroamerican burials in other cemeteries were not used.

For the most part, the Africans' coffins were made with iron nails rather than with more costly screws. Nails were commonly found in the graves, whereas screws were rare. Screws were used sparingly to strengthen corners or to secure the lids of a few coffins. Usually, only two or three screws were used to build a coffin, if used at all. Most of the screws found at the site came from hexagonal coffins, which could mean they were made by professional cabinetmakers.

Four coffins had traces of possible red-paint residue. This coloring was probably a primer. More expensive coffins of the time were often painted black. It could also be that the four coffins were painted black but that black paint decomposed in the ground, turning red over time. The residue could not be analyzed, so its origin remains uncertain.

Shrouds

Most people went to their graves in shrouds, burial cloths, or sometimes their street clothing. Most of this clothing or covering decomposed underground. Project archaeologists had to rely on metal objects that still remained, such as buttons and pins, to determine what types of clothing people were buried in. Shroud pins were found in more than two-thirds of the burials. These pins would have held together the fabric used to cover the dead. African women and children who sewed for European households could easily acquire pins for shrouds. In some burials, pins were found only near the head. These pins could have been used to secure a chin cloth to prevent the jaw from opening

Top, *Copper alloy straight pin as recovered in the field (photograph by Jon Abbott);* bottom, *replicas of African Burial Ground pins created by artisans at Colonial Williamsburg (photograph by Rob Tucher) (from* The Archaeology of the New York African Burial Ground, *Part 1).*

Pin with fabric from Burial 415. This burial held a man buried in clothing and with this pin and cloth on the cranium. Recovered during laboratory cleaning of the skeletal remains (photograph by Jon Abbott) (from The Archaeology of the New York African Burial Ground, *Part 1).*

Coffin Decoration

Most seventeenth-century coffins were simple, with no elaborate decoration, such as handles, cloth interior, or decorative tacks. By 1750, lid fasteners, handles, plates, and other decorations were available for people who could afford them. The lack of decoration on most coffins at the New York African Burial Ground could be a sign of poverty or that enslavers were unwilling to pay for extra decoration on coffins for the enslaved. An iron breastplate appears to have been used on only one coffin, the hexagonal coffin of a child 1–2 years of age (Burial 252). Only seven iron casket handles with back plates were unearthed, six of them on the coffin of a man aged 20–24 years (Burial 176). Four coffins were decorated with iron tacks or nails; all of those were for adult males buried after 1760. A 26–35-year old man (Burial 101), for instance, had a coffin adorned with a heart-shaped symbol outlined in tacks, which may suggest an Akan or West African identity for the deceased. The coffin lid of a man 35–40 years of age (Burial 332) was decorated with iron tacks. The tacks formed the initials "HW" and the number "38."

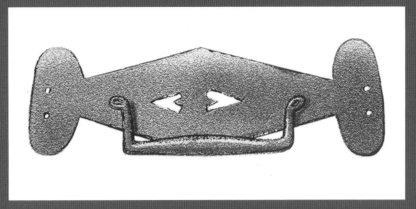

Composite drawing of coffin handle based on the X-rays taken of the handles from Burials 176 and 90 (drawing by C. LaRoche and R. Schultz).

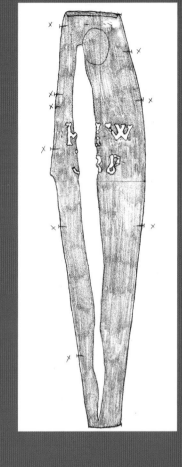

Burial 332 coffin lid, drawn as found during the excavation. The oval indicates where the skull was visible through the remnants of the coffin wood (drawing by M. Schur).

Left, photograph of Burial 332 coffin lid decoration formed of iron tacks; right, reconstruction of initials "HW" and number "38." The coffin lid had split longitudinally, severing the "H" and the likely "3" (photograph by Dennis Seckler).

All images on this page are from The Archaeology of the New York African Burial Ground, Part 1.

during burial. Another possibility is that pins were used to hold back the shroud to expose the face. Other burials had no evidence of street clothing or shroud pins. Those individuals could have been buried in winding sheets that were wrapped around the body. Such practices were known and common in Africa.

If the presence of pins is any guide, then around 69 percent of the individuals buried at the New York African Burial Ground were buried with shrouds. A typical shroud used by Europeans during the 1700s looked like a nightshirt that was open in the back and tied at the feet. African dead probably were shrouded no differently than Euroamericans. Many of the shrouded corpses at the burial ground site were those of women, children, and infants, but about half the males also wore shrouds. Shroud pins were uncommon for the burials that the researchers determined took place before 1735, but this may be because the earlier burials were less well preserved, and the pins may have deteriorated in the ground.

Personal Adornment

Few ornaments or pieces of jewelry were found with the dead at the New York African Burial Ground. Earrings and necklaces were worn as jewelry. A cast silver pendant that may have been worn as an earring was found near the jaw of a child (Burial 254). Copper-alloy rings were found in several burials.

Plain, copper-alloy ring from "Burial 398" (redeposited fill soil) (photograph by Jon Abbott) (from The Archaeology of the New York African Burial Ground, Part 1).

Plain, copper-alloy ring from Burial 71 (photograph by Jon Abbott) (from The Archaeology of the New York African Burial Ground, Part 1).

Copper-alloy ring with glass insets from Burial 242. Construction is cast metal; the ring band and face were cast as one unit. Each side has three faceted blue glass insets (photograph by Jon Abbott) (from The Archaeology of the New York African Burial Ground, Part 1).

Clothing and Buttons

Almost no fabrics survived with the remains unearthed from the New York African Burial Ground. Most of what we know about the clothing worn by the dead comes from buttons found in the burials. Sometimes, the position of the buttons was used to learn what kinds of clothing were worn. The position of buttons on a probable 25–30-year-old man (Burial 6), for instance, suggests he wore a button-down jacket. Most of the eight buttons on his jacket did not match and probably came from several different pieces of clothing before being used on his jacket. A man of 40–45 years (Burial 10) also wore a jacket. It was fastened with at least seven matching buttons.

Other buttons may have fastened the front of a pair of trousers, such as those found with a man of 20–23 (Burial 181) buried without a coffin. A 12–18-year-old of indeterminate sex (Burial 203) had eight wooden buttons that probably fastened a pair of breeches. A man aged 45–55 years (Burial 326) may have worn trousers held up by copper alloy buttons at the hips. So did a 42–52-year-old man (Burial 392), who had rows of buttons lying by his knees. A woolen buttonhole was also recovered from his grave.

All of the deceased seem to have been buried without shoes. Shoes were probably too valuable to bury with the dead. The mourners may have also believed that shoes should not be buried with the dead.

Copper-alloy ring with glass insets from Burial 310. Construction is cast metal; the ring band and face were cast as one unit. Each side had three faceted blue glass insets; one is missing. The central glass inset also is missing (photograph by Jon Abbott) (from The Archaeology of the New York African Burial Ground, Part 1).

Buttons from the New York African Burial Ground

Buttons from Burial 6 associated with a man's coat or jacket (photograph by Jon Abbott).

Gilt, copper-alloy button from Burial 6 (photograph by Jon Abbott).

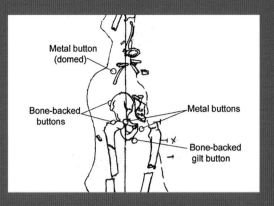

Detail of the disturbed Burial 181 with buttons in the pelvic area (drawing by M. Schur).

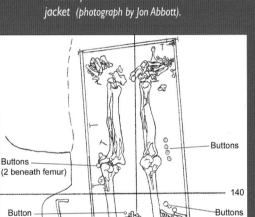

Detail of Burial 392 with buttons at knees and hips. This burial was oriented unusually with the head to the east (in situ drawing by M. Schur).

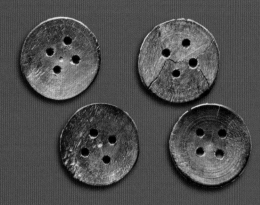

Bone buttons from Burial 392 (photograph by Jon Abbott).

Copper-alloy, with zinc and nickel, button from Burial 181 (photograph by Jon Abbott).

Copper-alloy button, with bone back, Burial 181 (photograph by Jon Abbott).

Copper-alloy button from Burial 181, (left) face; (right) back (photograph by Jon Abbott).

Bone button from Burial 392 (photograph by Jon Abbott).

Wool buttonhole from Burial 392 (photograph by Jon Abbott).

Bone and copper-alloy button from Burial 181: (left) back; (right) detail of flattened shank (photograph by Jon Abbott).

All images on this page are from The Archaeology of the New York African Burial Ground, Part 1.

89

Rings were worn on the fingers and, in some cases, may have been part of other ornaments. An adult woman aged 33–58 years (Burial 377) had three rings at her throat. These may have been part of a necklace. Four adult women aged from 25 to 52 (Burials 71, 115, 242, and 310) wore rings on the right or left hand. An adult of unknown sex (Burial 398) may have worn one also.

The most common form of ornament was glass beads. Yet only 146 glass beads and 1 amber bead were recovered from the graves. Almost all of them were made in Venice, an Italian city where glass trade beads had been made for centuries. Beads from Venice reached even the furthest interior of tropical Africa as well as North America and the Caribbean. A child 1.5–4 years of age (Burial 187) was buried with a string of 22 European-made black beads around the hips.

A few beads found in the burials were of a type made by West African glassmakers who recycled European glass to make new beads. They pounded the glass fragments into powder and placed them in small clay molds. They next placed a thin reed or manioc stem in the center of the mold to leave a hole for stringing. The mold was then fired in small kilns made of clay. Beads made in West Africa were found in only two burials, Burials 434 and 226. One white bead made in West Africa was found with Burial 434, a partially excavated grave. An infant less than 2 months of age (Burial 226) was buried with a strand of yellow beads made in West Africa. These were placed near the neck and may have been part of a necklace. A strand of waist beads and cowry shells was placed around the hips of an adult woman aged 39.3–64.4 years (Burial 340). The cowries and one of the beads, as well as the use of this kind of waist strand, are all of likely African origin.

Orientation

The standard burial orientation was with the head to the west for nearly 98 percent of graves. Christians often bury their dead with the head pointing west to allow the deceased to rise facing the east on the day of the Last Judgment. In the New York African Burial Ground, the most common orientation was 90° west of north, with considerable variation on either side.

Project archaeologists investigated what factors may have influenced the exact orientation of graves. They determined that one possibility was variation due to the changing points on the horizon where the sun sets through the year. Burials could have also been aligned with buildings, streets, or fences. The most prominent street near the burial ground was Broadway, which led travelers north out of the city.

Opaque redwood on transparent apple-green core bead from Burial 107 (photograph by Jon Abbott) (from The Archaeology of the New York African Burial Ground, Part 1).

Translucent light gold-colored beads from Burial 340 (photograph by Jon Abbott) (from The Archaeology of the New York African Burial Ground, Part 1).

Transparent light gray beads from Burial 428 (photograph by Jon Abbott) (from The Archaeology of the New York African Burial Ground, Part 1).

Beads from the New York African Burial Ground

Opaque black bead from Burial 250 (photograph by Jon Abbott).

Tubular or cylindrical opaque white bead from Burial 434 (photograph by Jon Abbott).

Barrel-shaped, opaque black bead from Burial 340 (photograph by Jon Abbott).

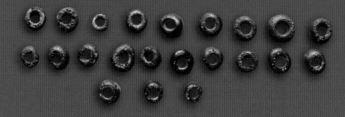

Donut-shaped to tubular opaque black beads from Burial 187 (photograph by Jon Abbott).

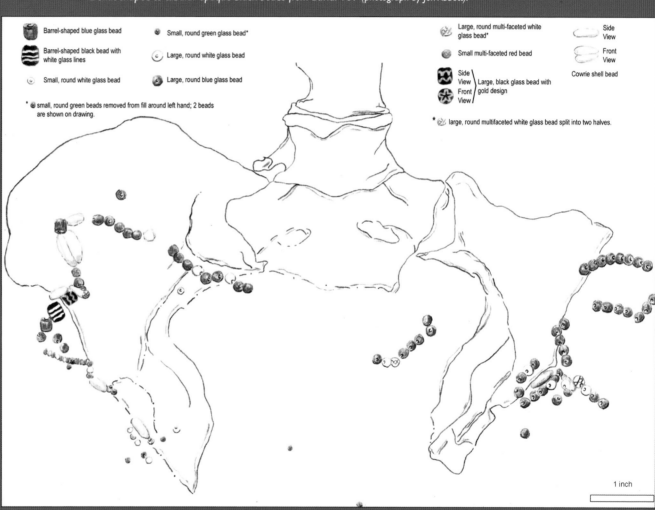

Barrel-shaped blue glass bead

Barrel-shaped black bead with white glass lines

Small, round white glass bead

Small, round green glass bead*

Large, round white glass bead

Large, round blue glass bead

Large, round multi-faceted white glass bead*

Small multi-faceted red bead

Side View / Front View, Large, black glass bead with gold design

Side View
Front View

Cowrie shell bead

* small, round green beads removed from fill around left hand; 2 beads are shown on drawing.

* large, round multifaceted white glass bead split into two halves.

1 inch

Drawing of Burial 340 showing location of possible waist beads (redrawn by M. Schur from photocopy of original field drawing).

All images on this page are from The Archaeology of the New York African Burial Ground, Part 1.

At least some of the burials were aligned perpendicular to Broadway. Later, buildings may have been used as a reference point to orient burials. Almost certainly, many of the graves were aligned with reference to their neighbors.

One area in the far eastern area of the excavation yielded some distinctive women's burials. Two women (Burials 383 and 365) were buried 10 feet apart with their heads to the south rather than the west. One of the women was of indeterminate age. The other was between 14 and 18 years of age. It is not known why they were oriented differently than other burials.

Shared Graves

Almost all the graves in the New York African Burial Ground burials contained only one individual—that is, a grave was dug and a coffin containing one person was placed at the bottom of a grave. The grave was then filled in with dirt. No mass graves were discovered during the excavations. Mass graves, or the burial of many individuals in the same grave, can be expected at burial grounds in times of infectious disease or war or as a result of executions. Apparently, African New Yorkers called attention to each person's individuality when they buried their dead. Twenty-seven graves, however, had multiple burials placed within them. In some cases, two or more coffins were placed in a single grave during the same burial event. In others, a second burial was placed in a grave after the grave had already been in use. Most shared graves were of children or infants buried together. Sometimes, children were placed above or immediately adjacent to adult burials. In a few cases, an infant lay at the foot of an adult grave. In other cases, newborn babies were buried within the coffin of an adult woman, either in a separate coffin or in the women's arms. Those burials could have represented a mother and child who died together or close in time.

Individual burial did not mean isolated interment, for most graves were within a foot or two of one another. From all indications, the New York African Burial Ground was African-controlled. Grouping of burials could reflect family or kinship ties, even common origin. Future studies of DNA may help determine who in the burial ground may have been related.

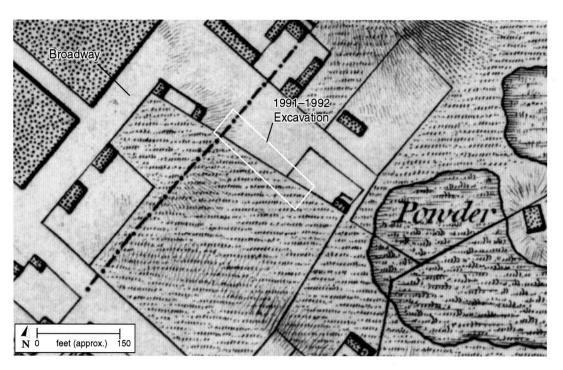

Site location overlaid on the Ratzer Map (1767). The solid line crossing the excavation site may represent the boundary between the cemetery/Van Borsum patent and the Calk Hook Farm at the time the map was made. The area containing excavated graves spanned this line. The dashed-dotted line parallel to Broadway is the ward boundary (Geography & Map Division, Library of Congress) (from The Archaeology of the New York African Burial Ground, Part 1).

Shared Graves

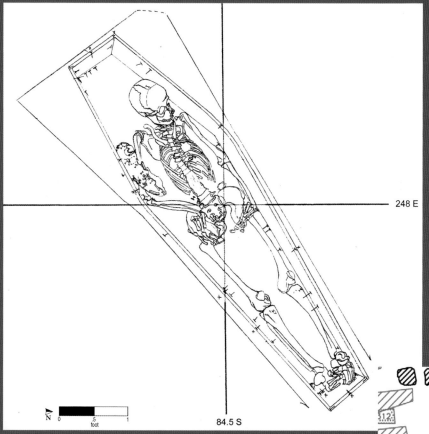

84.5 S

248 E

Burials 335/356 contained the remains of a woman between 25 and 35 years old (Burial 335) and a newborn infant (Burial 356). Researchers concluded that they were probably a mother and child who died during or soon after the infant's birth *(drawing by M. Williams) (from* The Archaeology of the New York African Burial Ground, *Part 2).*

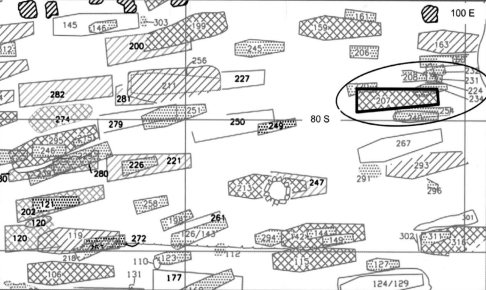

Detail of west-central portion of site plan showing all temporal groups. Note shared Burials 142, 144, and 149, bottom right, and Burials 202 and 121, bottom left. A possible shared burial (Burials 226 and 121) is located just left of center. Interestingly, the researchers noted a cluster of children's burials beneath Burial 207 (circled). Early Group burials are shown in color, with Late Group Burial 207 shown with coffin outlined in black *(from* The Archaeology of the New York African Burial Ground, *Part 1).*

Offerings

Unfortunately, the location of the original ground surface was not documented when the African Burial Ground was first excavated. This made it impossible later to identify offerings placed on graves or to identify faint traces of grave markers. Artifacts that may have been placed on top of gravesites could not be studied. Only those items placed in grave shafts or burials could be studied as possible offerings to the deceased.

During the seventeenth century, African societies placed goods in graves, such as pots, cowry shells, or metal tools, to help the deceased in the afterlife. Along with other clues, discovering such offerings can help archaeologists decipher a people's views of life after death. Many from West and West Central Africa believed that when people died they became ancestor spirits. Upon death, these ancestor spirits passed through water to live in the world of the dead. African diviners and healers often communicated with ancestral spirits to help in times of crisis or to learn who was causing problems for the living. Health problems and social problems were often thought to be caused by a lack of balance between the world of the living and that of the dead. The help of ancestor spirits was needed to fix problems in the world of the living. These spirits also needed to be provided with offerings of food, alcohol, and other items to keep them happy.

Very few burials at the New York African Burial Ground contained artifacts that could be interpreted as offerings. Items like coins, shells, pipes, and unusual artifacts were found in 26 burials. Some of these artifacts were probably personal possessions buried with the deceased. Nearly half of the graves with such artifacts date to after 1775, a time when many African fugitives from enslavement reached New York. Some of these individuals, many of whom fled to the city with just the clothes on their backs, may have been buried in their regular clothing, with personal possessions still in their pockets.

Other artifacts may have been placed deliberately in burials for a spiritual purpose. One adult man and two adult women, for example, had coins placed over their eyes. The adult man, aged 45–55 years old (Burial 214), had a coin and a knife near his left side, near the pelvis or forearm; perhaps they had been in his pocket. The practice of placing coins with the dead dates back to the ancient Greek tradition of providing a fare for Charon, the ferryman who carried the dead across the River Styx. Christian mourners placed coins on the eyes of the deceased in England and other European countries well into the twentieth century, as did many Africans in America.

Several clay tobacco pipes were found with the deceased. Pipe smoking was common among African New Yorkers of both sexes. Researchers noted that some individuals had notches worn into their teeth over time by holding a pipe stem between the teeth.

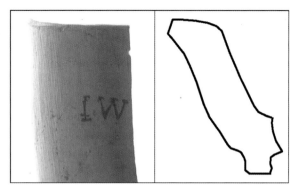

Left, *Detail of clay pipe bowl, showing IW mark, from Burial 158 (photograph by Christopher R. DeCorse); right, drawing of bowl shape (from* The Archaeology of the New York African Burial Ground, *Part 1).*

Photograph of clay pipe stem and bowl near the left forearm of Burial 165 (photograph by Dennis Seckler) (from The Archaeology of the New York African Burial Ground, *Part 1).*

Clay pipe stem and bowl from Burial 165 (photograph by Christopher R. DeCorse) (from The Archaeology of the New York African Burial Ground, *Part 1).*

African Diviners

African diviners and healers were among those enslaved and transported by force to the Caribbean and the Americas. They often carried pouches or bundles of special items that they used to communicate with the spirits. Called conjuring bundles, such bundles contained items that were symbolic of important energies, essences, or deities. Items in bundles were made of things like claws, teeth, clay, ash, nut shells, bird skulls, feathers, or roots. Each of these items held a specific spiritual meaning. Healers and other enslaved Africans also kept charms on their persons for protection or good luck. Several of the people who were buried at the African Burial Ground were buried with items that could have been parts of conjuring bundles or charms. A male aged 55–65 years (Burial 147) may have had part of a bundle or charm hidden in his sleeve. Protective amulets hidden on the upper body were common among West Africans of the day. A clay ball with a copper-alloy band was found in the burial of a young woman (Burial 375). Similar artifacts have not been found at other sites, but other researchers have described small clay balls used for luck or in divination rituals. The young woman's clay ball appeared to have been placed in a bag, which may have contained other items and could have been part of a conjuring bundle. Perhaps the woman, found buried without a coffin and with her arms crossed over her head, was a conjurer or diviner in life. She may have been lowered into the grave by holding her hands and feet, an uncommon form of burial in this part of the burial ground.

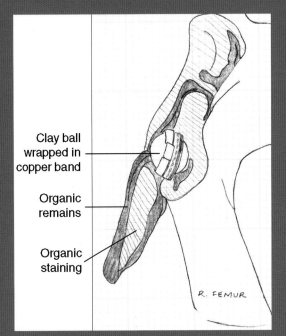

Clay ball wrapped in copper band

Organic remains

Organic staining

R. FEMUR

Drawing of artifacts at the hip of the woman in Burial 375 (drawing by M. Schur) (from The Archaeology of the New York African Burial Ground, *Part 1).*

Ceramic and copper-alloy sphere with band from Burial 375 (photograph by Jon Abbott) (from The Archaeology of the New York African Burial Ground, *Part 1).*

95

An unused clay pipe was placed under the hips of a woman aged 39.3–64.4 years (Burial 340). Her teeth showed no signs of previous pipe use, which could mean that the pipe was symbolic. Symbolic placement of tobacco pipes and knives has been noted in other burials of enslaved Africans in the Caribbean.

It is often difficult for archaeologists to know what artifacts meant to the people who used them. Further, many artifacts do not preserve well over time. Parts of coffins, clothing, or conjuring bundles at the burial ground site apparently decomposed over time. Only the hard, more durable parts remained. Knowing what is missing is often difficult. Also, some items found in burials were not intentionally placed in them. They were part of the natural environment or mixed into the soil from previous activity. For instance, ceramic sherds and pieces of animal bone were found in many grave shafts at the New York African Burial Ground. Some ceramic sherds may have been deliberately selected because they had designs on their surfaces that were similar to African symbols. Most sherds and animal bone were trash from the nearby tanneries and potteries. Oyster shell also found its way into graves by accident, because oyster shells were also discarded on the site.

Unused clay pipe from Burial 340 (photograph by Jon Abbott) (from The Archaeology of the New York African Burial Ground, *Part 1).*

Africans may have placed flowers in many graves. However, it is difficult to determine whether flowers were placed in graves, because the pollen that is used to identify flowers does not preserve well in wet and acidic soils. Project archaeologists took samples of pollen from several graves to see if flowers had been placed there. In some burials, pollen was not found. In other burials, pollen from wild flowers was preserved. The soil from the burial of a child aged 2.5–4.5 years old (Burial 45) yielded pollen from honewart, thorow wax, and carrot. These are all flowering plants that grow wild in the New York area. The grave of a man of 30–40 years (Burial 194) contained a high level of chicory pollen, suggesting that the man may have eaten chicory leaves shortly before his death. Another possibility is that chicory flowers were placed on his coffin.

Funeral Ceremonies

The New York African Burial Ground Project researchers know that African New Yorkers' funerals were not documented in any detail. Researchers do know from historical accounts that some African funerals in New York shared similarities with their counterparts in Africa. In Africa, ceremonies and beliefs varied among groups, but many involved drumming, chants, and dance. Bodies were often washed and prepared for burial by specially designated kin.

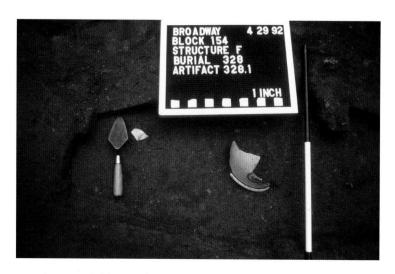

Photograph of stoneware vessel fragment that was probably deliberately placed with Burial 328 (photograph by Dennis Seckler) (from The Archaeology of the New York African Burial Ground, *Part 1) .*

Burial 214: Associated Items That Survived Over Time

Copper-alloy coin from Burial 214, which held a man between 45 and 55 years of age (photograph by Jon Abbott).

Knife handle, bone or antler and iron, from Burial 214 (photograph by Jon Abbott).

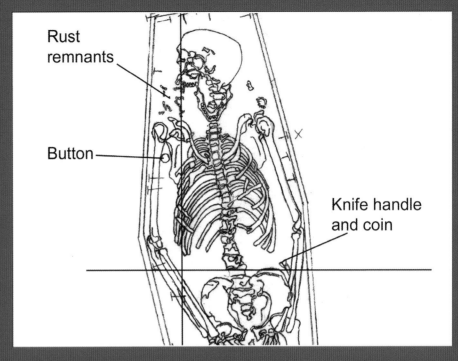

Rust remnants

Button

Knife handle and coin

Drawing of Burial 214, showing artifact locations (drawing by M. Schur).

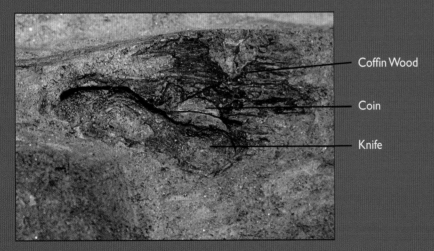

Coffin Wood

Coin

Knife

Photograph of knife handle from the left forearm area of Burial 214. The coin is visible above the right side of the knife handle, lying on a fragment of coffin wood (photograph by Dennis Seckler).

Copper-alloy button back from Burial 214: (left) front; (right) back (photograph by Jon Abbott).

Ceremonies could last for days or weeks before and after burial. Additional ceremonies were held after burial and took place at multiple locations. The rituals that gave meaning to the funerals held at the African Burial Ground are mostly lost, however. Nothing was recorded about these rituals or how they might have changed over time.

Some questions archaeologists have asked about Africans in the Americas are: How did enslavement affect the enslaved Africans' beliefs and practices? What did enslavement do to African identities? Many archaeologists have argued that Africans assimilated into the Euroamerican culture. In other words, they came to think and do things as the Euroamericans did. Other archaeologists have argued that Africans kept their African roots, but they changed by blending with Euroamerican, Native American, and other African cultures. As a result, African Americans developed many distinctive cultures in different parts of the Americas.

Many Africans were exposed to Christianity in Africa, the Americas, and the Caribbean. Some were even baptized or practiced some form of Christianity. For instance, many Kongolese were Catholic. They were not the same as European Catholics. Instead, they interpreted Christianity in terms of their own beliefs. Christianity was a thin coating over a core of Kongolese belief. In New York, many enslaved Africans attended church or bible classes. For a time, conversion to Christianity was a means to gain freedom, but freed or enslaved Africans were almost never full members of Christian society. By the 1700s, African burials were not allowed in New York church cemeteries, and few African New Yorkers were members of a Christian church. Teaching Christianity to Africans was also generally frowned upon.

Some burials at the New York African Burial Ground are similar to European Christian burials in their use of coffins, individual burials, and westward orientation. None of these practices means that Africans held Christian views of death. No definite evidence, like crosses, was found to suggest Christian belief on the part of mourners. Even if such artifacts had been found, they may not necessarily have had the same meanings for the enslaved Africans as they did for Europeans or Euroamericans.

At least some African New Yorkers likely would have practiced Islamic faiths, as West Africans were also exposed to Islam. Islam was present in West African kingdoms long before Europeans arrived on African shores. Like Christianity, Islam melded with traditional African beliefs. Muslims, however, were often buried on their right side, facing Mecca, without a coffin. Almost no burials in the burial ground suggest the practice of Islam. One individual may have been placed on his right side, but this is uncertain because the burial had been disturbed prior to the excavation.

Elias Neau's Catechism School

The Society for the Propagation of the Gospel in Foreign Parts established a school in the early 1700s to teach Christianity to enslaved Africans and Native Americans. The instructor, Elias Neau, held classes in his home on Wednesday and Friday evenings and on Sundays after church services. Many Africans attended Neau's classes to learn more about Christianity and to sharpen their reading skills. After the 1712 Uprising, several Euroamericans claimed that these classes led to rebellion among enslaved Africans. The classes continued to be held until Elias Neau's death in the 1720s, however. Few Africans who attended class were baptized, partly because few Euroamericans would sponsor African baptisms. Africans also had little incentive to be baptized, as it did nothing to change their enslaved status.

Christianity and Slavery

Early Europeans justified slavery as a way to bring "heathen" Africans to Christianity. They believed that dark-skinned people were impure and that light-skinned people were pure. Regardless, enslaved Africans who accepted Christianity and were baptized were seldom set free. The Dutch Reformed Church actively converted Africans to Christianity in the early years of Dutch settlement of the Americas. They stopped doing so in the 1650s, when they began importing enslaved Africans directly from Africa, because they feared that enslaved Africans only used Christianity to obtain their freedom, rather than to follow Christian virtues.

The British held the same view and made very few efforts to Christianize the Africans they enslaved. In the early 1700s, however, Elias Neau, a French-born New Yorker, held classes to convert Africans to Christianity. Many Africans attended, but permission was required for them to be baptized, and few enslavers gave such permission. Around the same time, a law was passed stating that religion could not be used as a reason to free enslaved Africans. Still, many Africans attended church services, but few were members, and when they were allowed to attend, they were kept separate from the rest of the congregation. Even the Quakers, who were against slavery, did not invite Africans into their churches. Many Africans kept their own spiritual beliefs and made sense of Christianity in terms of their own backgrounds. By the end of the 1700s, many African Christians had split off from European congregations and started their own churches, such as the African Methodist Episcopal Zion Church, established in 1795.

The African Methodist Episcopal Zion Church at Tenth and Bleecker Streets in New York City, built in 1864. From the time the church was originally established in 1796, it was instrumental in securing new areas for New York African burials after the closing of the African Burial Ground (The Picture Collection of the New York Public Library).

A. M. E. ZION CHURCH,
CORNER OF WEST TENTH AND BLEECKER STREETS, NEW YORK CITY.

It is possible that Africans of Islamic or other faiths were buried in different parts of the burial ground, but not in the area that was excavated.

An African American Institution

Based on what the project archaeologists found, the Africans buried in the part of the New York African Burial Ground that was excavated buried their dead in much the same way. The basic pattern appeared early on and continued for a century or more. The African community or a portion of that community must have been close knit and conservative for this to occur. No matter how much their backgrounds varied, and no matter how much time passed, they did some things the same way every time. Although the project area reflects a part of the larger community, it is simply unknown how similar that area is to other areas of the burial ground.

What is certain is that the enslaved Africans' African identities were not lost in New York. People of many different African backgrounds were present in New York, and they routinely gathered to share their African heritages. African funerals were run by Africans. The provision of a coffin seems to have been the only involvement of their enslavers. Clothing styles, ornaments, and coffin decoration unearthed with their graves suggest that enslaved Africans were poor. Ornaments and decoration, which would have been costly for people with so little, were provided when possible. Some items—like beads, shells, and pieces of reflective material—suggest a broad base of African belief. Other items that could have provided clues to African heritages possibly were left on the ground surface, and these have not survived.

Burials speak of relationships to family and kin and also to a wider community. Death and burial were fundamental rites of passage for a community that was always striving to maintain its own identity. As the African Burial Ground was used and incorporated newcomers from many cultures, it became an institution that lived on in African churches of the 1800s. At the burial ground, African New Yorkers made and maintained their own sacred space. They performed funerals and visited the graves of loved ones when they could. The burial ground was one of the few places in New York where enslaved African men, women, and children were allowed to act together and on each other's behalf. Clearly, they buried their loved ones with care and respect. Ceremonies at graveside and afterward insisted on recognizing the full humanity of the deceased. Their enslavers, however, increasingly covered the burial ground with trash, and the space got smaller and smaller over time as the city grew around it. Still, the African Burial Ground never lost its importance to the people who used it and whose ancestors were buried there.

African Spiritual Meanings

Some artifacts placed in burials hint at African spiritual meanings. Several graves yielded seashells such as clams and oysters. A child 2.5–4 years of age, for example, wore a shell as a necklace (Burial 22). Shells may have symbolized the passage between the realm of the living and the dead, which many African groups associated with water. Artifacts made from shell and a piece of iron were placed on the lids of three coffins, as if placed there as offerings. It is unknown what these artifacts were or what they meant, but it may be that both the shell and the iron material had symbolic meaning. In Yorubaland, beads, shell, iron bars, and other items were and are associated with a deity of the sea named Olokun. Coral offerings were found, too. A 45–60-year-old man (Burial 376) was buried with a piece of coral found mainly in the Caribbean. Materials that looked like water or flashes of light were used to communicate with spirits. Due to their shiny, reflective appearance, such items were called "flashes." A small, shiny disk made of micaceous schist, for example, was found in the burial of a man aged 30–40 years (Burial 135). Due to its shiny appearance and worked edges, this artifact may have been a flash. Other items found in burials included a calcite crystal placed with a 3–5-year-old child (Burial 55), a small glass sphere in the burial of a woman of unknown age (Burial 410), and a rose quartz disk in the burial of a 5–9-year-old child (Burial 289).

Artifacts from the New York African Burial Ground

Coral (Siderastrea siderea) from Burial 376 (length is approximately 2.5 inches, or about 63 mm) (photograph by Dennis Seckler).

Mica schist disk from Burial 135 (diameter is 6 mm) (photograph by Jon Abbott).

Calcite-crystal cluster from Burial 55 (width is 3.5 mm) (photograph by Jon Abbott).

Rose quartz disk from Burial 289 (diameter is 7 mm) (photograph by Jon Abbott).

Glass sphere from Burial 410 (diameter is 3.44 mm) (photograph by Jon Abbott).

All images on this page are from The Archaeology of the New York African Burial Ground, Part 1.

THE IMPORTANCE OF THE AFRICAN BURIAL GROUND

CHAPTER 7

The African Burial Ground was used by thousands of Africans who were among the earliest inhabitants of what became New York City. Their efforts and their presence helped to build and shape the city. A sacred place, the burial ground was the final resting place of many who, against their will, were taken from their homelands and enslaved in a far-away place. Their children, who were enslaved upon birth, also were laid to rest there. The contributions of these enslaved Africans were almost forgotten, but now, through the study of this hallowed site, they are known and remembered.

Beginning in 1991, the remains of more than 400 individuals were removed from the burial ground. Many members of the public did not like the idea of removing the remains. Once the project was reorganized by the GSA and the descendant community and Howard University became involved, however, the project began to address the public's concerns. The excavations were stopped, and the GSA's building plans were altered. The responsibility for studying the site was placed in the hands of noted experts on the African Diaspora. Howard University, an institution with unparalleled experience in that field of study, was given scientific control of the project. Howard's leadership served to assure the public that Americans would have the opportunity to learn as much as possible about the lives of their African ancestors, whose history had been all but forgotten.

The story of the African Burial Ground is one that must be told and remembered again and again. It is a story of slavery and racism. It is a story of workers whose forced labor was the foundation of a major American city's life. It is also a story of triumph and hope. Despite slavery, early African New Yorkers' beliefs and practices lived on and formed a central part of their African American identities. African New Yorkers buried their dead according to their own traditions and survived as a people. They contributed new forms of song, dance, art, and communication, and developed new skills and new traditions with African roots. Above all, African New Yorkers maintained their human dignity.

The Sankofa symbol of the Twi-speaking Akan-Asante people of West Africa illustrates the meaning of the proverb, "Se wo were fi na wo sankofa a yenkyi," or "It is not a taboo to return and fetch it when you forget." As Sankofa embodies the need to remember one's ancestors and to tie the past with the present to better prepare for the future, the New York African Burial Ground researchers speculated that its possible presence on the coffin of Burial 101 might be evidence of the portability of culture from Africa to the New World. It also reinforced for them the importance of cultural remembrance for the survival of African people throughout the Diaspora (from The Archaeology of the New York African Burial Ground, Part 1).

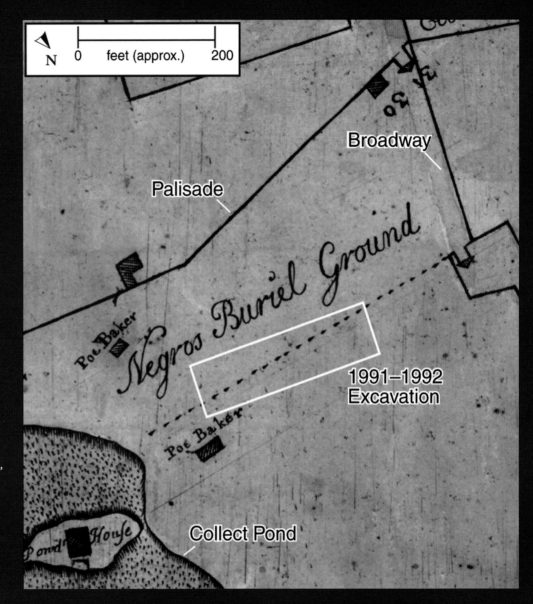

The map to the left shows the site location overlaid on the Maerschalk Plan, which was drawn in 1754 when it was still known as the "Negros Buriel Ground." The site has since been renamed the African Burial Ground at the request of the descendant community (Geography & Map Division, Library of Congress) (from The Archaeology of the New York African Burial Ground, *Part 1).*

When the African Burial Ground was rediscovered, African Americans of the twentieth and twenty-first centuries fought once again for their seventeenth-century ancestors' dignity. Because of the descendant community's requests and demands, proper respect was paid to the people buried in the burial ground.

The African Burial Ground is a symbol of the struggles and contributions of African New Yorkers. In 1994, former mayor of New York City, David Dinkins wrote:

> Millions of Americans celebrate Ellis Island as the symbol of their communal identity in this land. Others celebrate Plymouth Rock. Until a few years ago, African-American New Yorkers had no site to call our own. There was no place which said, we were here, we contributed, we played a significant role in New York's history right from the beginning . . . . Now we—their descendants—have the symbol of our heritage embodied in lower Manhattan's African Burial Ground. The African Burial Ground is the irrefutable testimony to the contributions and suffering of our ancestors.

Reburial

By 2003, the laboratory analysis of the New York African Burial Ground remains and artifacts was complete. Every artifact had been thoroughly studied, and all the data were stored in project databases. The remains were ready to be placed back into the ground. The descendant community had fought hard to ensure that these ancestors would be properly reinterred where they had once rested.

The reburial ceremonies were planned and carried out by the Schomburg Center, the U.S. Army Corps of Engineers, and the GSA. In October 2003, the human remains and artifacts were reburied at the New York African Burial Ground. All were placed in beautifully carved walnut and cedar coffins specially made in Ghana for the ceremony. The artifacts placed in each coffin were only those clearly associated with the individual burials when they were excavated. Trash from nearby industries in the excavated dirt was not reburied. If anything, the researchers concluded, those artifacts had desecrated the burials and would not be returned to the soil of the burial ground.

For the reburial ceremonies, four individuals were chosen to symbolize the people who had been buried at the African Burial Ground: an adult male, an adult female, a male child, and a female child. Together, these four individuals traveled in a special procession from Washington, D.C., to New York City. The procession stopped in major cities along the way where enslaved Africans had toiled. Upon their arrival at Wall Street in New York City, the four individuals led a procession of carriages carrying the coffins.

Wooden coffins, hand-carved in Ghana, held the ancestors' remains for reburial at the New York African Burial Ground (photograph by Anne and Jon Abbott) (from The Archaeology of the New York African Burial Ground, Part I).

Mother Delois Blakely sits proudly atop the wagon leading the October 2003 procession of mostly African American descendant community members marking the return of their ancestors' remains and artifacts to the New York African Burial Ground. More than 400 wooden coffins, hand-carved in Ghana, West Africa, were constructed to return the bodies to their original, sacred place of rest for proper reburial after completion of the Howard University-headed laboratory analysis (from The Archaeology of the New York African Burial Ground, Part 1).

The procession traveled up Broadway to the burial ground site, which had once been on the outskirts of the city. A vigil was held through the night. The following day, a final ceremony was conducted, and the coffins were lowered reverently into the ground.

Completing the Research

The New York African Burial Ground researchers spent several more years analyzing and interpreting what they had learned. They spent thousands of hours trying to understand the lives people lived and how they were treated in death. It was a unique opportunity to understand the incredible hardships that African New Yorkers had endured and the equally incredible triumphs they had achieved. Learning what these ancestors had faced was a painful and moving experience for all the researchers.

The combination of researchers and methods from the fields of history, skeletal biology, and archaeology provided a deeper understanding of enslaved lives in colonial New York City. Still, as project scientist Cheryl LaRoche and Scientific Director Michael Blakey wrote: "Archaeology is not an end in itself. For many African Americans, it is a conduit, an avenue leading to spiritual rebirth and renewal of our history. Our history is in the bones and in the artifacts excavated from the African Burial Ground."

With the publication of this book, the reporting is complete, but the research continues. Digital images, photographs, slides, videos, project documents, and artifacts that were not reburied are now cared for by the Schomburg Center for Research in Black Culture where they will remain available for future research. A limited number of samples from bones and teeth that were used for isotope, DNA, and trace element analysis and that were not reburied are cared for at the W. Montague Cobb Laboratory at Howard University. Large amounts of data collected in the laboratory and at archives and libraries in Africa, Europe, the Caribbean, and the United States await interpretation. Other data and findings are currently being used to understand other African Diaspora sites. DNA studies have allowed African Americans to learn more precisely where in Africa they and their families originated. Through science and the pursuit of truth, the legacy of the New York African Burial Ground Project lives on and will endure into the future.

The Importance of the African Burial Ground

The African Burial Ground is important to many people on many levels. It is important to African Americans and people of African descent throughout the world as a symbol of their struggle, humanity, and respect for the ancestors. The burial ground is also

The Memorial

At the behest of the African American descendant community in New York, the U.S. government built a memorial to the New York African Burial Ground, which was completed in 2007. The memorial was designed by architect Rodney Léon, an African American of Haitian descent. Graced with African symbols, it is based on circle and spiral motifs typical of many African cultures. Symbols remind the visitor of the circle of life, the return to origins, and the need to remember one's past. The memorial is an expression of the ties that bind the past, present, and future. An inscription on the wall of the memorial describes its purpose, proclaiming to all who visit that it is:

> For all those who were lost
> For all those who were stolen
> For all those who were left behind
> For all those who are not forgotten

Visitors to the memorial follow a spiral path that descends below ground and circles a map of Africa, Europe, and the Americas. The path symbolizes the passage from the secular to the sacred, emphasizing the spiritual power of the site. The center and origin of the spiral is West and West Central Africa, the region where many African New Yorkers and their ancestors had been born. The memorial provides a sacred space for individual contemplation, reflection, meditation, and prayer as well as space for public cultural ceremonies and sacred rituals. Congressman Charles B. Rangel of New York's 15th Congressional District has stated:

> This beautiful memorial is of national and international significance for those of us who are African Americans as well as other people of African descent worldwide. It will stand as a permanent symbol of our caring and concern that our ancestors buried here receive their just recognition and respect.

The African Burial Ground Memorial located at Duane and Elk Streets in Manhattan. Note the Sankofa symbol visible on the entry wall (courtesy U.S. General Services Administration, Carol M. Highsmith Photography, Inc.).

important to national and global history. It tells a forgotten story about slavery, racism, and oppression in New York and the contributions of Africans to the building of the United States. It tells a difficult and painful story of the connections between Europe, Africa, and the Americas in the making of the United States and the modern world.

Recently, Mark Leone, Cheryl LaRoche, and Jennifer Babiarz wrote that the New York African Burial Ground Project "has had a profound impact not only on the interested public but on the archaeological community as well." They maintain that, because of that groundbreaking research, archaeologists now regularly include descendants in the study of African Diaspora sites and human remains and make better use of experts in African Diaspora studies. Further, new ways to study the origins and life experiences of Africans in the diaspora were pioneered by the researchers, who exposed the many flaws with racialized approaches to studying skeletal biology and African American history.

The New York African Burial Ground Project has altered some of the fundamental conclusions about what happened to African identities in the Americas. Archaeologists can no longer conclude that Africans simply lost or abandoned their cultural roots while enslaved and became part of the dominant culture. Their identities instead remained rooted in Africa and became part of new African-style traditions in the Americas. Nor can it be claimed any longer that slavery was absent from America's northern colonies. The research showed that slavery was part of every aspect of daily life in New York for centuries. It affected everything and everyone. Moreover, the conditions of slavery caused serious health problems and early deaths for enslaved Africans. Worse still, even after slavery ended, the racism that went hand-in-hand with it, in both the North and the South, never died.

New York's troubled past can no longer be forgotten. The New York African Burial Ground Project has educated the public on the role of slavery in New York and the contributions of Africans to the making of New York City. It has shown the world where those African New Yorkers came from, how they got to New York, and what happened to them along the way. It tells us about the lives they led in lower Manhattan and what they did to fight slavery and racism and maintain their dignity. Finally, it tells us about how these ancestors died and how they were treated in death. Their names will never be known, but through the study of bones, artifacts, and documents, parts of their stories have been told, and the New York African Burial Ground is once again a sacred place.

Visiting the African Burial Ground

The African Burial Ground National Monument, declared by President George W. Bush on February 27, 2006, is under the stewardship of the National Park Service. The associated visitors center and memorial tell the story of African people in New York City, their struggle for freedom, and their immense contributions to the city and the nation. Visitors to the monument can view exhibits and replica artifacts at the visitors center. Visitors can learn more about the African presence in New York City by taking scheduled or self-guided tours in the neighborhood of the burial ground site. For more information on hours and visiting the memorial, go to the National Park Service Web site at http://www.nps.gov/afbg.

Unearthed *is a sculpture of three individuals from the New York African Burial Ground. Left, the 20–24-year-old woman in Burial 25, who was found with a musket ball lodged in her rib cage; middle, the 26–35-year-old man in Burial 101, who had the possible Sankofa symbol on his coffin lid; and right, the 50–60-year-old woman in Burial 89, one of the oldest individuals recovered from the burial ground. Sculpted in bronze by world-renowned sculptor Frank Bender, the sculpture was made by reconstructing the age, sex, and facial features of the three individuals, based on information obtained from studying their bones.*

UNEARTHED
FRANK BENDER
2002

Commissioned for the United States by the
General Services Administration and the
British Broadcasting Company to memorialize
the African Burial Ground in New York City.

GLOSSARY

Africans: One of the ethnic groupings present in colonial New Amsterdam and New York. The Africans came from the areas of West and Central Africa and Madagascar via the Caribbean Island and Brazil.

Anthropology: (from the Greek *anthropos = man* and *ology = the study of*). The study of humans in terms of physical characteristics and culture in order to explain why we behave as we do. The field is usually divided into four sub-fields: archaeology, physical anthropology, cultural anthropology, and anthropological linguistics.

Archaeological site: A location exhibiting evidence of past human activity.

Archaeology: The study of past human cultures based on the interpretation of material remains (such as artifacts and features), studied in conjunction with: alterations in the natural landscape (such as landfill), written records, informants' accounts (information supplied by people who have either lived during the time being studied or can repeat an oral history), and ethnographic analogy (explaining past practices based on observations of contemporary practices).

Artifact: Objects made or altered by humans (e.g., such as tools and other implements, household goods, clothing, etc.) often recovered in fragmentary form.

Assimilate: To absorb a group into the culture and lifeways of a dominant group.

Biocultural anthropology: The scientific study of the relationships between human biology, culture, and history.

Chipping: The removal of flakes of material from an object, such as a stone, bone, or tooth, by carefully striking or placing pressure on the edge of the material with another object.

Coffin hardware: Items such as nails and handles associated with a coffin (or casket).

Cribra orbitalia: A condition that causes the bone around the eye sockets to appear pitted and spongy. Cribra orbitalia could result from nutritional problems.

Cultural anthropology (ethnology): The study of present-day cultures. Archaeologists studying the African Burial Ground use the research of cultural anthropologists whose field of interest has been African studies in order to explain cultural data found in the burial ground. The records of cultural anthropologists may be supplemented by the writings of travelers.

Cultural feature: A structure or group of artifacts (for example, refuse deposits, building remains, etc.) created by people.

Cultural resources: Physical evidence of our history, culture and heritage, including buildings, cemeteries, archaeological sites, etc.

Cultural resources management: The practice of managing, interpreting and protecting cultural resources, such as archaeological sites, buildings, or artworks in response to various laws enacted in the late 1960s and 1970s.

Culture: The sum of ideas, behaviors, and artifacts relative to a specific group of people for a specific time period.

Curation: The process of managing and preserving an archaeological collection of artifacts and records according to professional museum and archival practices.

Demography: The study of the population structure of groups, including such characteristics as age and gender.

Descendant community: Those individuals who could have ancestors among the people who used or created an archaeological site.

Distal: The end of an object that is furthest away from the point where it originates or attaches to another object.

DNA: Deoxyribonucleic acid (DNA) is the genetic material found in all organisms and some viruses. A kind of code or blueprint, DNA contains the instructions used in the development and functioning of an organism.

Dutch: The people of the Netherlands (present day Holland) were the first Europeans to colonize New York (then called New Amsterdam). The Dutch settlers were composed of several different ethnic groups, including the Walloons.

Ethnography: The scientific description of cultural groups from an anthropological perspective. Ethnography is often accomplished through living with the group under study and participating in their daily activities.

Ethnohistory: The historical and anthropological study of specific ethnic groups.

Forensic anthropology: The reconstruction of human identity (age, gender, ancestry, etc.) based on the study of human tissue after death.

Genetics: The scientific study of the inheritance and expression of traits in living organisms.

Grave shaft: A grave pit dug during interment in which the deceased is placed.

Historical archaeology: The branch of archaeology studying past cultures with written records or documentary evidence, usually applied to American archaeology after 1492.

In situ: (from Latin) In place. In archaeology, in situ refers to the original position of an artifact or other remains as they were found in the ground or on the ground surface.

Interment: A burial.

Isotope: Different types of atoms of the same chemical element. For a particular element, isotopes have the same number of protons, but a different number of neutrons. Different isotope ratios, or signatures, are distinctive for certain kinds of foods or geographic regions.

Lesions: Abnormal tissue, such as on a bone or tooth, that resulted from disease or injury.

Manumission: Granting freedom from enslavement.

Micaceous schist: A kind of rock, formed in layered sheets, which is especially shiny due to the presence of crystallized mica minerals.

Mortality: The number or proportion of deaths in a given time or place.

Musculoskeletal stress markers: Places on the skeleton where muscle attachments are overdeveloped or damaged.

Native Americans: The first peoples to inhabit the Americas, and their descendants, believed to have entered by a land bridge that once connected present-day Siberia and Alaska. The Native American residents of what is known today as New York City, Long Island and Westchester were speakers of the Algonquin language; hence they are often called Algonquin. The group of Algonquins from the area of New Amsterdam and eastern New Jersey are the Lenape. The other major Native American language spoken in New York State was Iroquoian, whose people are known as the Iroquois or Six Nations. Most Native American place names in the New York City area are of Algonquin origin. Manhattan, for example, is suggested to mean "hilly island," a reference to the landscape of Manhattan during the colonial period.

New Amsterdam: The first European colony established on the southern tip of Manhattan. The colony was founded by the Dutch West India Company in 1624 to serve as a trading post. Animal furs were acquired from Native Americans in the Hudson Valley, brought to New Amsterdam, and then shipped to Holland.

Osteology: The study of bones, including their dimensions and chemical composition, providing anthropologists with information on the life of individuals in terms of age, gender, stature, diet, health, disease, ancestry, etc.

Patent: A parcel of land given or sold through an official agency, such as the government, or in the case of colonial New Amsterdam, the Dutch West India Company. A patent bestows upon the property owner (the patentee) legal right to the land.

Physical anthropology: The study of the physical make-up of the human being. This field is usually divided into evolution, genetics, and human variation.

Pinkster: A spring festival held in June, from the Dutch word *Pinksteren*, meaning "Pentecost." Originally a Dutch religious holiday, African New Yorkers celebrated Pinkster as a day away from work that could be spent sharing their culture and history with family and friends.

Plan drawing: Detailed record that provides overview and elevation of cultural features, including shape and size, as well as location according to the site grid and elevation above or below ground.

Porotic hyperostosis: A condition seen on the outer surface of bone that causes bone to appear pitted and spongy. Porotic hyperostosis is thought to result from nutritional problems, unsanitary living conditions, or both.

Pottery: A facility that makes objects out of clay, such as pots, by heating the formed clay to high temperatures in an oven, or kiln.

Prehistoric archaeology: The study of cultures existing before the advent of writing.

Provenience: The physical location where cultural materials are found, including elevation above or below ground (vertical space), and in relation to longitude and latitude (horizontal space).

Soil sample: Soil collected during excavation that is analyzed in a laboratory. A soil sample from the garden of a house may contain the seeds of what had been growing there. A soil sample from the region of the pelvis of a skeleton may contain evidence of an individual's diet.

Strontium isotope: An isotope of the chemical element strontium.

Tannery: A facility that makes leather from animal hides, which is often accomplished by using an acidic chemical compound called "tannin."

Temporal: Of or relating to time, such as a specific period of time or a sequence of time periods.

Walloons: The major ethnic group comprising the early Dutch settlers in New Amsterdam. They were French speaking Protestants from the Spanish Netherlands (present-day southern Belgium). The Walloons had long sought refuge in the Netherlands to escape religious persecution before coming to the Americas.

Ward: A division, or part, of a city created for administrative purposes, such as taxation or voting. Often, different wards might be characterized by different types of industry or land uses.

RECOMMENDED READING AND SOURCES

THE THREE TECHNICAL VOLUMES IN THIS SERIES

Blakey, Michael L., and Lesley M. Rankin-Hill (editors)

2009   *Skeletal Biology of the New York African Burial Ground.* The New York African Burial Ground: Unearthing the African Presence in Colonial New York, vol. 1, pt. 1. Howard University, Washington, D.C.

2009   *Skeletal Biology of the New York African Burial Ground: Burial Descriptions and Appendices.* The New York African Burial Ground: Unearthing the African Presence in Colonial New York, vol. 1, pt. 2. Howard University, Washington, D.C.

Medford, Edna Greene (editor)

2009   *Historical Perspectives of the African Burial Ground: New York Blacks and the Diaspora.* The New York African Burial Ground: Unearthing the African Presence in Colonial New York, vol. 3. Howard University, Washington, D.C.

Perry, Warren R., Jean Howson, and Barbara A. Bianco (editors)

2009   *The Archaeology of the New York African Burial Ground.* The New York African Burial Ground: Unearthing the African Presence in Colonial New York, vol. 2, pt. 1. Howard University, Washington, D.C.

2009   *The Archaeology of the New York African Burial Ground: Descriptions of Burials.* The New York African Burial Ground: Unearthing the African Presence in Colonial New York, vol. 2, pt. 2. Howard University, Washington, D.C.

2009   *The Archaeology of the New York African Burial Ground: Appendices.* The New York African Burial Ground: Unearthing the African Presence in Colonial New York, vol. 2, pt. 3. Howard University, Washington, D.C.

BOOKS

Berlin, Ira

1998   *Many Thousands Gone: The First Two Centuries of Slavery in North America.* Belknap Press of Harvard University Press, Boston.

Berlin, Ira, and Leslie M. Harris (editors)

2005   *Slavery in New York.* New Press, New York.

Cantwell, Anne-Marie, and Diana diZerega Wall

2001   *Unearthing Gotham: The Archaeology of New York City.* Yale University Press, New Haven.

Conniff, Michael L., and Thomas J. Davis (editors)

1994   *Africans in the Americas: A History of the Black Diaspora.* St. Martin's Press, New York.

Foote, Thelma Wills

2004   *Black and White Manhattan: The History of Racial Formation in Colonial New York City.* Oxford University Press, Oxford.

Goodfriend, Joyce D.

1992   *Before the Melting Pot: Society and Culture in Colonial New York City, 1664–1730.* Princeton University Press, Princeton, New Jersey.

Harris, Leslie M.

2003   *In the Shadow of Slavery: African Americans in New York City, 1626–1823.* University of Chicago Press, Chicago.

Hodges, Graham Russell

1999   *Root & Branch: African Americans in New York & East Jersey, 1613–1863.* University of North Carolina Press, Chapel Hill.

Hodges, Graham Russell, and Alan Edward Brown

1994   *"Pretends to Be Free": Runaway Slave Advertisements from Colonial and Revolutionary New York and New Jersey.* Garland, New York.

McManus, Edgar

1966   *A History of Negro Slavery in New York.* University of Syracuse Press, Syracuse.

Rothschild, Nan A.

1990   *New York Neighborhoods: The 18th Century.* Academic Press, New York.

Articles

Blakey, Michael L.
1998   The New York African Burial Ground Project: An Examination of Enslaved Lives, a Construction of Ancestral Ties. *Transforming Anthropology* 7(1):53–58.

2001   Bioarchaeology of the African Diaspora in the Americas: Its Origins and Scope. *Annual Review of Anthropology* 30:387–422.

Dunlap, David
1992   Unfree, Unknown: Buried Slaves Near City Hall. *New York Times*, December 26.

Frankel, Bruce
1992   Black Cemetery in New York City, New Key to Colonial Times. *USA Today*, September 15.

Franklin, Maria, and Larry McKee
2004   African Diaspora Archaeologies: Present Insights and Expanding Discourses. *Historical Archaeology* 38(1):1–9.

Harrington, Spencer P. M.
1993   Bones and Bureaucrats: New York's African Cemetery, Anatomy of an Excavation. *Archaeology Magazine*, March/April.

LaRoche, Cheryl J., and Michael L. Blakey
1997   Seizing Intellectual Power: The Dialogue at the New York African Burial Ground. *Historical Archaeology* 31(3):84–106.

Mack, Mark E., and Michael L. Blakey
2004   The New York African Burial Ground Project: Past Biases, Current Dilemmas, and Future Research Opportunities. *Historical Archaeology* 38(1):10–17.

Masters, Brooke A.
1992   Old Bones Promise a Wealth of Insight: Howard University Receives a Grant to Preserve, Study Nearly Unique Collection of Skeletons. *Washington Post*, August 3.

Orser, Charles E., Jr.
1998   The Archaeology of the African Diaspora. *Annual Review of Anthropology* 27:63–82.

Rankin-Hill, Lesley M., and Michael L. Blakey
1994   W. Montague Cobb (1904–1990): Physical Anthropologist, Anatomist, and Activist. *American Anthropologist* 96(1):74–96.

Shipp, E. R.
1992   Black Cemetery Yields Wealth of History. *New York Times*, August 9.

Documentary Films

Kutz Television, Inc.
1994   *The African Burial Ground: An American Discovery.* Parts I–IV. VHS. Written by Christopher Moore and directed by Anna Switzer. National Technical Information Services, National Audiovisual Center, Springfield, Virginia.

Volume 1, *Skeletal Biology of the New York African Burial Ground*

Michael L. Blakey, Ph.D.

Dr. Blakey served as the scientific director of the New York African Burial Ground Project. He has also served as a curator of the W. Montague Cobb Human Skeletal Collection while a professor of Anthropology and Anatomy at Howard University. His scholarly publications concern the history and philosophy of science, paleopathology, historical demography, medical anthropology, racism, museums, and anthropological ethics. His papers appear in such journals as *American Anthropologist*, *American Journal of Physical Anthropology*, *International Journal of Anthropology*, and *Critique of Anthropology*.

Dr. Blakey is currently at the College of William and Mary as a National Endowment for the Humanities professor and serves as the director of the Institute's Historical Biology program. He attended Howard University and the University of Massachusetts, where he received a Ph.D. in Anthropology. Dr. Blakey has also received an honorary D.Sc from New York College, City University of New York.

Lesley Rankin-Hill, Ph.D.

Dr. Rankin-Hill was a principal researcher and the associate editor for the skeletal biology volume of the African Burial Ground Project. She has also served as co-director for Oral History Project 5, which represents a unique model for the documentation of community history by Latino youths in Washington DC. Her publications include *A Biohistory of 19th-Century Afro-Americans* (1997).

Dr. Rankin-Hill is currently an associate professor of anthropology and women's studies at the University of Oklahoma. Her research focus includes physical and medical anthropology, and biochemistry of the African Diaspora, Latinos and Afro-Americans. She received her Ph.D. in anthropology from the University of Massachusetts-Amherst.

Volume 2, *The Archaeology of the New York African Burial Ground*

Warren Perry, Ph.D.

Dr. Perry served as the associate director and principal archaeologist for the African Burial Ground Project since 1993. He has engaged in other archaeological excavations both in the United States and in Africa including an archaeological study in Staten Island, New York (1990s); in Swaziland (1980s and 1990s); and the New Salem Plantation Archaeological project, and the Connecticut Minkisi project. His book titled *Landscape Transformation and the Archaeology of Impact* (1999), presents his findings in the Swaziland study.

Dr. Perry joined the faculty of Central Connecticut State University in 1993 as an assistant professor and now serves as the director of the Archaeology Laboratory for African and African Diaspora Studies. Dr. Perry attended New York University and the City University New York, where he received a Ph.D. in Anthropology.

Jean Howson, Ph.D.

Dr. Howson served as the associate archaeology director for research and excavation for the African Burial Ground Project. Since 1995, she has served as the principal archaeologist of the RBA Group, Inc., as well as a member of the board of the Atlantic Highlands Historical Society responsible for conducting initial inventory of west side historic houses.

Dr. Howson is a recipient of the Fulbright-Hays fellowship, and her academic and teaching work includes lectures at Rutgers University, New York University, and Vassar College. Her publications include: "Social Relations and Material Culture: A Critique of the Archaeology of Plantation Slavery" (1990) (in Historical Archaeology on Southern Plantations and Farms, edited by Charles E. Orser. *Historical Archaeology* 24(4):78–91). Dr. Howson received a bachelor's degree from Vassar College and Ph.D. in Anthropology from New York University.

Barbara Bianco, Ph.D.

Dr. Barbara Bianco served as research associate for archaeology of the African Burial Ground Project. She has lectured in the Archaeology department at Vassar College, and her publications include a chapter in *Rethinking pastoralism in Africa: gender, culture & the myth of the patriarchal pastoralist,* edited by Dorothy L. Hodgson, (2000). Dr. Bianco holds a Ph.D. degree in Anthropology from New York University.

Volume 3, *Historical Perspectives of the African Burial Ground: New York Blacks and the Diaspora*

Edna Greene Medford, Ph.D.

Dr. Medford served as the Director for History of New York's African Burial Ground Project since 1996. Her publications include the coauthored work *The Emancipation Proclamation: Three Views* (2006), and she has published more than a dozen articles and book chapters on African Americans, especially during the era of the Civil War.

Dr. Medford attended Hampton Institute (VA), the University of Illinois (Urbana), and the University of Maryland (College Park), where she received her Ph.D. in history. She is currently an Associate Professor and former director of the Department of History's graduate and undergraduate programs at Howard University. Her teaching specialty includes nineteenth-century African American history, the Civil War and Reconstruction, Colonial America, and the Jacksonian Era.

CONTRIBUTORS TO *SKELETAL BIOLOGY OF THE NEW YORK AFRICAN BURIAL GROUND*

PROJECT DIRECTOR AND SCIENTIFIC DIRECTOR

Michael L. Blakey, Ph.D.

LABORATORY DIRECTOR AND OSTEOLOGIST

Mark E. Mack, M.A.

OFFICE MANAGER AND ADMINISTRATIVE ASSISTANT

Reba Brewington, B.A.

OSTEOLOGIST

M. Cassandra Hill, M.A., Ph.D.*

OSTEOLOGICAL TECHNICIANS

Autumn Barrett, M.A. A.B.D.*
Allison Davis
Reynard Davis (deceased)
Ena Fox
Shannon Mahoney, M.A., A.B.D.*
Susan Good-Null, M.A., Ph.D.*
Monde Imoh, Ph.D.
Christopher Null, M.A., A.B.D.*
Kenya Shujaa, M.A.*
Rachel Watkins, M.A., Ph.D.*

OSTEOLOGICAL TECHNICIAN ASSISTANTS

Valarian Abrams
Paula Allen
Marc Alston
Darious Annis
Augustus Billy
Alan Blanc
Antonia Christian

Jeffrey Coleman
Lauren Collins
Cyndi Douglas Jacinta Elder-Arrington
Nardos Fessaha, Ph.D.*
April Flint
Gabriel Franke, M.A.
Paul Gattis
Oumuyiwa Gbadegesin
Richlyn Goddard, Ph.D.
Karyn Goodwin
Yasin Gregg
Janna Gruber
Fayola Herod
Michael Hunter
Keisha Hurst
Joseph Jones, M.A.*, A.B.D.*
Antoinette Kearney
Irina Koretsky, M.S.
Dannette Lambert
Teresa Leslie, M.A.,* Ph.D.*
Arion Mayes, M.A., Ph.D.*
Moses Nwulia
Auriel Perkins
Keisha Rankine
Clifford Russell
Joann Sampson
Jobita Smith
Azhar Talibi, M.A., M.D.*
Brent Terry, M.A.
Emile Webster
Shani Wright

RESEARCH ASSISTANTS

Pamela Brown
Songhai Carter
Christa Dickey
Lesley Payne
Arana Hankin
Nicole Harvey
Jeffrey Lim
Chad Taylor
Walidah West

SENIOR MEDICAL PHOTOGRAPHER

Otto Edwards

DATA SYSTEMS MANAGER

Douglas Fuller, M.A.
Javier Urcid, Ph.D.
Christopher Null

SECRETARIES

Denise Joseph
Marna Lewis
Andrea Reid
Raquel Scott
Percival Taylor
Sharon Wiltshire

BOTANISTS

Lafayette Frederick, Ph.D.
Monde Emoh, Ph.D.

CONSULTANTS FOR THIS REPORT

Richard Kittles, Ph.D.
Matthew George, Ph.D.
Thomas Stafford, Ph.D.
Shomarka O.Y. Keita, M.S., M.A., M.D.

AFRICAN BURIAL GROUND PROJECT DIRECTORS

Michael L Blakey, Ph.D., Scientific Director, College of William and Mary, and Howard University
Edna Medford, Ph.D., Associate Director for History, Howard University
Sherrill D. Wilson, Ph.D., Director, Office of Public Education and Interpretation
Alan H. Goodman, Ph.D., Associate Director for Chemical Studies, Hampshire College
Jean Howson, Ph.D., Archaeology Laboratory Director, Howard University
Fatimah L. C. Jackson, Ph.D., Associate Director for Genetics, University of Maryland
Mark E. Mack, M.A., Cobb Laboratory Director, Howard University
Warren Perry, Ph.D., Associate Director for Archaeology, Central Connecticut State University
Lesley M. Rankin-Hill, Ph.D., Associate Director for Skeletal Biology, University of Oklahoma
Warren Barbour, Ph.D., Associate Director (1992–1994)

AFRICAN BURIAL GROUND PROJECT ADMINISTRATION/ MANAGEMENT

O. Jackson Cole, Ph.D., Executive in Charge, Howard University
James A. Donaldson, Ph.D., Project Manager, Howard University

*Degree received post-recordation.

CONTRIBUTORS TO ARCHAEOLOGY OF THE NEW YORK AFRICAN BURIAL GROUND

DIRECTOR FOR ARCHAEOLOGY

Warren R. Perry, Ph.D., Central Connecticut State University

ASSOCIATE DIRECTOR FOR ARCHAEOLOGY

Jean Howson, Ph.D.

LABORATORY DIRECTOR

Leonard G. Bianchi, M.A.

RESEARCH ASSOCIATE

Barbara A. Bianco, Ph.D.

HISTORICAL AND ARCHAEOLOGICAL CONSULTANTS

E. Kofi Agorsah, Ph.D., Portland State University
Steven Barto, M.A., M.L.S., New York Municipal Archives
Christopher R. DeCorse, Ph.D., Syracuse University
Augustin F. C. Holl, Ph.D., University of Michigan at Ann Arbor
Meta F. Janowitz, Ph.D.

RESEARCH ASSISTANTS

Shannon Mahoney, M.A.
Ruth Mathis, M.A.
Janet L. Woodruff

ARCHAEOLOGICAL TECHNICIANS

Jean-Marie Cerasale
Tarik Holmes
Tamara Kelly
Iciar Lucena Narvaez
Allison Manfra
Amy Page

Paula Saunders
Cristine Whibby

DIGITAL MAPPING

Robert Bethea, M.A.
Marques Roberts
Percival Taylor, M.A.
Ed Zeltmann, The RBA Group

FAUNAL AND FLORAL ANALYSTS

Patricia Fall, Ph.D., Arizona State University
Gerald K. Kelso, Ph.D.
Lisa Lavold-Foote, Arizona State University
Marie-Lorraine Pipes
Leslie Raymer, R.P.A., New South Associates

ADVISORY REVIEW BOARD

Francis P. McManamon, Ph.D., RPA, Chief Archaeologist, National Park Service
Theresa A. Singleton, Ph.D., Syracuse University
Diana diZerega Wall, Ph.D., City University of New York City College

AFRICAN BURIAL GROUND PROJECT DIRECTORS

Michael L. Blakey, Ph.D. (College of William and Mary), Scientific Director
Edna Greene Medford, Ph.D. (Howard University), Director for History
Warren R. Perry, Ph.D. (Central Connecticut State University), Director for Archaeology
Sherrill D. Wilson, Ph.D., Director, Office of Public Education and Interpretation
Lesley M. Rankin-Hill, Ph.D. (University of Oklahoma), Director for Skeletal Biology
Alan H. Goodman, Ph.D. (Hampshire College), Director for Chemical Studies

Fatimah L. C. Jackson, Ph.D. (University of Maryland), Director for Genetics
Jean Howson, Ph.D., Associate Director for Archaeology
Leonard G. Bianchi, M.A., Archaeology Laboratory Director
Mark Mack, M.A. (Howard University), Cobb Laboratory Director

AFRICAN BURIAL GROUND PROJECT ADMINISTRATION/ MANAGEMENT

O. Jackson Cole, Ph.D. (Howard University), Executive in Charge
James A. Donaldson, Ph.D. (Howard University), Project Manager

CONTRIBUTORS TO *HISTORICAL PERSPECTIVES OF THE AFRICAN BURIAL GROUND:*
NEW YORK BLACKS AND THE DIASPORA

DIRECTOR OF AFRICAN BURIAL GROUND HISTORY COMPONENT

Edna Greene Medford, Ph.D. (Howard University)

CONTRIBUTING AUTHORS

Emilyn L. Brown, M.A. (Independent Researcher)
Selwyn H. H. Carrington, Ph.D. (Howard University)
Linda Heywood, Ph.D. (Boston University)
Edna Greene Medford, Ph.D. (Howard University)
John Thornton, Ph.D. (Boston University, Consultant)

RESEARCHERS

Allison Blakely, Ph.D. (Boston University)
Emilyn L. Brown, MA (Independent Researcher)
Selwyn H. H. Carrington, Ph.D. (Howard University)
Michael Gomez, Ph.D. (New York University)
Linda Heywood, Ph.D. (Boston University)
Jean Howson, Ph.D. (Independent Researcher)
Edna Greene Medford, Ph.D. (Howard University)
Arnold Taylor, Ph.D. (Emeritus Professor, Howard University)
John Thornton, Ph.D. (Boston University)
Jeanne Toungara, Ph.D. (Howard University)

GRADUATE STUDENT RESEARCHERS

Miranda Booker
Roger Davidson, Ph.D.*
Milagros Denis*
Lisa Y. King, Ph.D.*
Talitha LeFlouria
Learie Luke, Ph.D.*
Wendi Manuel-Scott, Ph.D.*
Habib Warmack
Charles Wash*

Erika Watkins
Louis Woods*

UNDERGRADUATE ASSISTANTS

Ana Cardoso (Howard University Ronald McNair Scholar)
Rashauna Johnson (Howard University Ronald McNair Scholar)
Tiffany Johnson (Howard University Ronald McNair Scholar)
Lark Medford (Howard University Volunteer)
Moja Mwaniki (Howard University Ronald McNair Scholar)
Natalie Richardson (Howard University Ronald McNair Scholar)
Marlena Skinner (Howard University Work Study Student)
Benjamin Talton, Ph.D.* (Howard University Ronald McNair Scholar)

SPECIAL ASSISTANCE

Sherrill Wilson, Ph.D. (Office of Public Education and Information, New York's African Burial Ground Project)
Sheila Walker, Ph.D. (Spelman College)
Trevor Hall, Ph.D. (Northern Caribbean University)
Jean-Michel Makebo-Tali, Ph.D. (Howard University)

ILLUSTRATOR

Michael Colbert

AFRICAN BURIAL GROUND PROJECT ADMINISTRATION/MANAGEMENT

O. Jackson Cole, Ph.D., Project Executive Officer
    Executive Assistant to the President, Howard University
James A. Donaldson, Ph.D., Project Manager
    Dean, College of Arts and Sciences, Howard University

* Degree awarded after assignment completed with African Burial Ground Project.

ILLUSTRATION CREDITS

The majority of the illustrations used in this volume originally appeared in the first three technical volumes of this series, *The New York African Burial Ground: Unearthing the African Presence in Colonial New York.*

Volume 1, Part 1: Skeletal Biology of the New York African Burial Ground

Volume 1, Part 2: Skeletal Biology of the New York African Burial Ground: Burial Descriptions and Appendices

Volume 2, Part 1: Archaeology of the New York African Burial Ground

Volume 2, Part 2: Archaeology of the New York African Burial Ground: Descriptions of Burials

Volume 2, Part 3: Archaeology of the New York African Burial Ground: Appendices

Volume 3: Historical Perspectives of the African Burial Ground: New York Blacks and the Diaspora

CHAPTER 1

Page 2: Location of African Burial Ground archaeological excavation site in lower Manhattan, New York (Volume 2, Part 1, Figure 28). (New York City Mapped Street: Section 12—Borough of Manhattan, New York County; used with permission of the New York City Department of City Planning. All rights reserved.)

Page 3: **Top left,** *Burial 12* (Volume 1, Part 2: Page 9). **Middle left,** *Enslaved domestic laborers in eighteenth-century New York* (Volume 3, Figure 16; illustration by Michael Colbert, 2004). **Bottom left,** *Construction during archaeological fieldwork* (Volume 2, Part 1, Figure 6; photograph by Dennis Seckler). **Right,** *The Directory Plan of 1789, showing the city just before the closing of the African Burial Ground* (Volume 2, Part 1, Figure 23; Geography & Map Division, Library of Congress).

Page 4: Backhoe clearing adjacent to temporary archaeological excavation shelter early in the fieldwork (Volume 2, Part 1, Figure 3; photograph by Dennis Seckler).

Page 5: **Top,** *Night procession of "The Ties That Bind" ceremony in November 1993* (Volume 1, Part 1, Figure 8; photograph by Roy Lewis). **Bottom,** *Chief Alagba of New York, commemorating the ancestors at the New York African Burial Ground* (Volume 2, Part 1, Epilogue; photograph by Dennis Seckler).

Page 6: *Mayor David Dinkins, Peggy King Jorde (Mayor's Liaison), and Howard Dodson (Chief, Schomburg Center) are briefed on the excavation by Michael Parrington (Principal Archaeologist for HCI and John Milner Associates)* (Volume 1, Part 1, Figure 7).

Page 7: **Top left,** *Drawing of Burial 147, showing three pins aligned along the inside of the right upper arm* (Volume 2, Part 1, Figure 272; drawing by M. Schur). **Bottom left,** *Copper-alloy rings from Burial 147* (Volume 2, Part 1, Figure 273; photograph by Jon Abbott). **Right,** *The complete drawing of Burial 147, including the coffin outline, site and grid lines, and locations of artifacts on different parts of the skeleton* (Volume 2, Part 2: Page 197; drawing by M. Schur).

Page 9: **Top left,** *Project Director Michael Blakey and Data Systems Manager Douglas Fuller discuss organization of the database* (Volume 1, Part 1, Figure 11). **Top right,** *Osteological Technician Assistant Joseph Jones involved in cleaning and reconstruction* (Volume 1, Part 1, Figure 14). **Bottom,** *Comparative male and female pelvic shapes* (Volume 1, Part 1, Figure 16).

Page 11: **Top,** *Example of a digital photographic series of an artifact* (Volume 2, Part 1, Figure 8; photographs by Jon Abbott). **Bottom left,** *Photograph of Burial 22* (Volume 2, Part 1, Figure 263; photograph by Dennis Seckler). **Bottom right,** Clamshell fragment on coffin lid of Burial 348 (Volume 2, Part 1, Figure 264).

Page 12: **Left,** *Allison Davis and Keisha Hurst take anthropometric measurements* (Volume 1, Part 1, Figure 15). **Right,** *Laboratory Director Mark Mack conducts dental recordation* (Volume 1, Part 1, Figure 27).

Page 13: **Top,** *Archaeologists working under lights* (Volume 2, Part 1, Figure 5; photograph by Dennis Seckler). **Bottom,** *Excavation shelter erected to allow night and winter work* (Volume 2, Part 1, Figure 4; photograph by Dennis Seckler).

CHAPTER 2

Page 15: *Detail of the Manatus Map, depicting New Amsterdam in 1639* (Volume 2, Part 1, Figure 10; Geography & Map Division, Library of Congress).

Page 17: Gezicht op Nieuw Amsterdam, *an early picture of ships leaving and arriving at New Amsterdam* (by Johannes Vingboons, 1664).

Page 18: *Contemporary artist's depiction of New York Africans building a structure* (illustration by Michael Colbert, 2004).

Page 19: Dutch-era land grants, superimposed on a Manhattan street grid (ca. 1835), showing the approximate locations of patents issued to African men and women (Volume 2, Part 1, Figure 13). (Source, Stokes [1915–1928(6):Plates 84B-a and 84B-b]. On the creation of the map, see Stokes [1915–1928(2):355–357]).

Page 20: Contemporary artist's depiction of New York Africans loading a ship (Volume 3, Figure 13; illustration by Michael Colbert, 2004).

Page 21: The 1740 Carwitham Plan (Volume 2, Part 1, Figure 16; Viscount Coke and the Trustees of the Holkham Estate).

Page 23: Auction of an enslaved man during the Dutch Period (Volume 3, Figure 4; Harper's Monthly Magazine, 1895).

Page 25: Execution on the Common (Volume 3, Figure 21; from Valentine 1860).

Page 26: Perimortem fractures of the humerus and femora in a female aged 18–20 years (Burial 205) (Volume 1, Part 1, Figures 129 and 130).

Page 27: **Left,** Photograph of Burial 25 during excavation (Volume 2, Part 1, Figure 84; photograph by Dennis Seckler). **Top right,** Musket ball lodged in rib cage of the woman in Burial 25 (Volume 2, Part 1, Figure 83; photograph by Dennis Seckler). **Bottom right,** Spiral fracture in lower arm of Burial 25 (Volume 1, Part 1, Figure 133).

Page 29: **Top left,** Excavated grave of Burial 18 with stone marker in place at its west (head) end (Volume 2, Part 1, Figure 58; photograph by Dennis Seckler). **Middle left,** Marker for Burial 23 in relation to nearby lines of cobbles (Volume 2, Part 1, Figure 61; photograph by Dennis Seckler). **Bottom left,** Vertical slab of stone found above Burial 47 (Volume 2, Part 1, Figure 59; photograph by Dennis Seckler). **Top right,** Stone that appears to have been a marker for Burial 23 (Volume 2, Part 1, Figure 60; photograph by Dennis Seckler). **Bottom right,** Burials at the southwest corner of the excavated cemetery that were marked with cobbles at the surface (Volume 2, Part 1, Figure 57; photograph by Dennis Seckler).

Page 31: New Yorker David Grim's recollection of the city in 1742–1744 (Volume 2, Part 1, Figure 18; The Lionel Pincus and Princess Firyal Map Division, The New York Public Library, Astor, Lenox and Tilden Foundations).

Page 33: **Top left,** In situ drawing of Burial 259 showing button locations (Volume 2, Part 1, Figure 182; drawing by M. Schur). **Bottom left,** Button with associated cloth and removed to show the buttonhole (Volume 2, Part 1, Figure 189; photograph by Jon Abbott). **Top right,** Copper-alloy buttons, with parallel ridged and milled decoration (Burial 259 (Volume 2, Part 1, Figure 183; photograph by Jon Abbott). **Middle upper right,** Tin-plated, copper-alloy button from Burial 259 (Volume 2, Part 1, Figure 184; photograph by Jon Abbott). **Middle lower right,** Textile from Burial 259, retrieved from coffin wood sample (Volume 2, Part 1, Figure 188; photograph by Jon Abbott). **Bottom right,** Possible leather-covered wood buttons from Burial 259 (Volume 2, Part 1, Figure 186; photograph by Jon Abbott).

Page 35: **Left,** Inset from the project site plan showing Burials 314 and 338 side by side (Volume 2, Part 1, inset of Figure 87d). **Right,** Burial 338, which held a 33-65-year-old woman, was buried side by side with Burial 314, which held a 40-50-year-old man (Volume 2, Part 2, Pages 458 and 420; drawings by M. Schur).

CHAPTER 3

Page 36: The Maerschalk Plan, 1754 (Volume 2, Part 1, Figure 19; Geography & Map Division, Library of Congress).

Page 37: Sanborn Map (Manhattan Land Book 1984-85) of New York's civic center area (Volume 2, Part 1, Figure 28) (use of 1984-85 Sanborn Map 290 Broadway, New York, NY, reprinted/used with permission from the Sanborn Library, LLC).

Page 38: The Van Borsum Patent, issued in October 1673 (Volume 2, Part 1, Figure 14). (New York State Archives; Series #A1881-78, Dutch Colonial Administrative Records Box 3, Vol. 3, part 3 pp 433–20. Von Borsum Patent.)

Page 39: **Left,** The Lyne-Bradford Plan depicts New York in 1730 (Volume 2, Part 1, Figure 15; Rare Books Division, The New York Public Library, Astor, Lenox and Tilden Foundations). **Top right,** Sherd from grave shaft of Burial 353 (Volume 2, Part 3, Appendix F:Plate F.37a). **Bottom right,** Pottery sherds from grave shaft of Burial 333 (Volume 2, Part 3, Appendix F:Plate F.33).

Page 40: **Top,** The Castello Plan, mapmaker Jacques Cortelyou's street grid of New Amsterdam in 1660 (Volume 2, Part 1, Figure 11; I. N. Phelps Stokes Collection, Miriam and Ira D. Wallach Division of Art, Prints and Photographs, The New York Public Library, Astor, Lenox and Tilden Foundations). **Bottom,** View of Trinity Churchyard, October 2005 (Volume 2, Part 1, Figure 12; photograph by Rob Tucher).

Page 41: Mrs. Buchnerd's hand-drawn Plan of the City of New York, 1735 (Volume 2, Part 1, Figure 17; I. N. Phelps Stokes Collection, Miriam and Ira D. Wallach Division of Art, Prints and Photographs, The New York Public Library, Astor, Lenox and Tilden Foundations).

Page 42: Detail of a petition submitted in June 1795 by the African Society (Volume 2, Part 1, Figure 25; courtesy New York City Municipal Archives; Papers of the Common Council, Petitions [Isaac Fortune, June 19, 1795]).

Page 43: **Left,** Taylor-Roberts Plan (1797) (Volume 2, Part 1, Figure 26; The Lionel Pincus and Princess Firyal Map Division, The New York Public Library, Astor, Lenox and Tilden Foundations). **Right,** Detail from a 1787 surveyor's map (Volume 2, Part 1, Figure 22; courtesy of the Division of Land Records [Liber 46:140]).

Page 44: Detail of the southwestern portion of the site plan showing all temporal groups (Volume 2, Part 1, Figure 71).

Page 45: **Top left,** Copper coin (George II halfpenny) from Burial 135 (Volume 2, Part 1, Figure 257; photograph by Jon Abbott). **Bottom left,** X-rayed copper George II halfpenny from Burial 135 and 1749 George II halfpenny from University of Notre Dame Libraries (Volume 2, Part 1, Figure 258; X-ray by Metropolitan Museum of Art, supplied by John Milner Associates). **Right,** Photograph of Burial 242, showing a copper coin in the left eye socket (Volume 2, Part 1, Figure 262; photograph by Dennis Seckler).

Page 46: **Left,** Drawing of Burial 35 (Volume 2, Part 2: Page 48; drawing by T. Gray). **Right,** Drawing of Burial 23 (Volume 2, Part 2: Page 23; drawing by C.S.G.).

Page 47: Top left, *Possible reading of the year "1769" formed by tacks on the lid of Burial 101 (Volume 2, Part 1, Figure 91; drawing by M. Schur).* **Middle left,** *Coffin lid decoration formed of iron tacks in Burial 101 (Volume 2, Part 1, Figure 90; photograph by Dennis Seckler).* **Bottom left,** *One version of the West African Sankofa symbol (Volume 2, Part 1, Figure 286).* **Right,** *Drawing of skeletal remains in Burial 101 (Volume 2, Part 1, Figure 92; drawing by M. Schur).*

CHAPTER 4

Page 49: *Major regions of Africa from the seventeenth and eighteenth centuries (Volume 1, Part 1, Figure 32).*

Page 50: *West Central Africa, Kongo-Angola Region (Volume 3, Figure 3). (Adapted from Warfare in Atlantic Africa, 1500–1800, John Thornton, ©1999, UCL Press. Reproduced by permission of Taylor & Francis Books UK.)*

Page 51: Top left, *The Senegambia Region, West Africa (Volume 3, Figure 7). (Adapted from Warfare in Atlantic Africa, 1500–1800, John Thornton, ©1999, UCL Press. Reproduced by permission of Taylor & Francis Books UK.)* **Bottom left,** *The Bight of Benin and Niger Delta, West Africa (Volume 3, Figure 9). (Adapted from Warfare in Atlantic Africa, 1500–1800, John Thornton, ©1999, UCL Press. Reproduced by permission of Taylor & Francis Books UK.)* **Right,** *The Gold Coast and Slave Coast, West Africa (Volume 3, Figure 8). (Adapted from Warfare in Atlantic Africa, 1500–1800, John Thornton, ©1999, UCL Press. Reproduced by permission of Taylor & Francis Books UK.)*

Page 52: Top left, *Elderly woman 50–60 years of age (Burial 40) (Volume 1, Part 1, Figure 24).* **Top right,** *Calf bones of woman 50–60 years of age (Burial 40) (Volume 1, Part 1, Figure 114).* **Bottom,** *Raster ablation of upper right first molar of Burial 23 (Volume 1, Part 1, Figure 46).*

Page 53: *Kongo woman laboring in agricultural field (Volume 3, Figure 11; courtesy of University of Arizona Special Collections, from Relation historique de l'Ethiopie occidentale; contenant la description des royaumes de Congo, Angolle et Matamba, by Giovanni Cavazzi, 1732).*

Page 54: *New York African Burial Ground skull shape analysis (Volume 1, Part 1, Figure 34).*

Page 55: Top, *Model showing how elements are deposited in teeth (Volume 1, Part 1, Figure 40).* **Bottom,** ^{87}*Strontium to* ^{86}*Strontium in samples of enamel and dentine of individuals from the New York African Burial Ground, plus two individuals from Ghana; water from Ghana; and an intrusive pig molar (Volume 1, Part 1, Figure 48).*

Page 56: *Dental modification of maxillary central incisors (Volume 1, Part 1, Figure 63).*

Page 57: Top left, *Photograph of Burial 340, showing beads (Volume 2, Part 1, Figure 67; photograph by Dennis Seckler).* **Middle left,** *Deep blue beads from Burial 340 (Volume 2, Part 1, Figure 232; photograph by Jon Abbott).* **Bottom left,** *Decorated and amber beads from Burial 340 (Volume 2, Part 1, Figure 238; photograph by Jon Abbott).* **Center,** *Simple black bead from Burial 340 (Volume 2, Part 1, Figure 233; photograph by Jon Abbott).*

Top right, *Translucent blue-green and opaque beads from Burial 340 (Volume 2, Part 1, Figure 231; photograph by Jon Abbott).* **Middle right,** *Possibly translucent amber beads from Burial 340 that developed a coating over time (Volume 2, Part 1, Figure 237; photograph by Jon Abbott).* **Bottom right,** *Cowry shell from Burial 340 (Volume 2, Part 1, Figure 244; photograph by Jon Abbott).*

Page 59: *A Liverpool Slave Ship, about 1780, by William Jackson (© National Museums Liverpool [The International Slavery Museum]).*

Page 60: *Regions where enslaved Africans were first shipped during the seventeenth and eighteenth centuries (Volume 1, Part 1, Figure 33).*

Page 61: *Divining the cause of death, an African funeral rite practiced in Jamaica (Volume 3, Figure 19; from Phillipo 1843).*

Page 62: *The Market House (Volume 3, Figure 17; from Bruce 1898).*

Page 63: *An early depiction of Africans and Europeans dancing at the marketplace (Volume 3, Figure 18; from Our Firemen: A History of the New York Fire Departments, Volunteer and Paid, from 1609 to 1887, by Augustine Costello).*

CHAPTER 5

Page 65: Top left, *Men's everyday breeches (Volume 2, Part 1, Figure 136; Colonial Williamsburg Collection, the Colonial Williamsburg Foundation).* **Middle left,** *Quilted petticoat (1770–1775) (Volume 2, Part 1, Figure 138; Colonial Williamsburg Collection, the Colonial Williamsburg Foundation).* **Bottom left,** *Self-enclosed casing for a drawstring, on a gown with set-in sleeves (1800–1810) (Volume 2, Part 1, Figure 140; Colonial Williamsburg Collection, the Colonial Williamsburg Foundation).* **Right,** *Working woman's striped linen wool petticoat (1770–1820) (Volume 2, Part 1, Figure 137; Colonial Williamsburg Collection, the Colonial Williamsburg Foundation).*

Page 66: *Ropewalk, a colonial industry where enslaved laborers worked (Volume 3, Figure 14; from Bridenbaugh 1950).*

Page 67: *The Townsend MacCoun Map (Volume 3, Figure 1; courtesy the New York Public Library Map Division).*

Page 68: *Typical kitchen in a colonial household where Africans lived and worked (Volume 3, Figure 15).*

Page 69: Top, *Severe hypertrophy in a male aged 40–50 years (Burial 369) (Volume 1, Part 1, Figure 121).* **Middle,** *Hypertrophy in a male aged 17–18 years (Burial 174) (Volume 1, Part 1, Figure 125).* **Bottom,** *Hypertrophy in a female aged 25–35 years (Burial 223) (Volume 1, Part 1, Figure 126).*

Page 70: *Cribra orbitalia of the left eye orbit (Burial 6, 25–35-year-old male) (Volume 1, Part 1, Figure 96).*

Page 71: Top left, *Porotic hyperostosis in 3–5-year-old child (Burial 138) (Volume 1, Part 1, Figure 93).* **Bottom left,** *Thickened diploe of 35–45-year-old male (Burial 151) compared with a normal specimen (Volume 1, Part 1, Figure 95).* **Top right,** *Porotic hyperostosis in a*

4.5–10.5-month-old child (Burial 64) (Volume 1, Part 1, Figure 94). **Bottom right,** *Cribra orbitalia of the right orbit of a 5–7-year-old child (Burial 39)* (Volume 1, Part 1, Figure 97).

Page 72: **Top,** *Indicators of infection on the right femur of a 50–60-year-old male (Burial 32)* (Volume 1, Part 1, Figure 88). **Bottom,** *Indicators of infection on the right femur of a 50–60-year-old male (Burial 32), magnified* (Volume 1, Part 1, Figure 89).

Page 73: *Lead variation* (Volume 1, Part 1, Figure 49).

Page 74: **Top,** *Indicators of infection on a 35–45-year-old male, magnified (Burial 70)* (Volume 1, Part 1, Figure 77). **Bottom,** *Indicators of infection on an adult male (Burial 69)* (Volume 1, Part 1, Figure 78).

Page 75: **Top,** *Bands of discoloration caused by hypocalcification in a 24–32-year-old female (Burial 51)* (Volume 1, Part 1, Figure 58). **Bottom left,** *Linear enamel hypoplastic lesions in a female aged 20–25 years (Burial 1)* (Volume 1, Part 1, Figure 57). **Bottom right,** *Deciduous mandibular dentition with a single non-linear hypoplastic pit in a child aged 3–5 years (Burial 7)* (Volume 1, Part 1, Figure 59).

Page 76: *Scant remains of the infant in Burial 226 with eight fired-glass beads worn at the neck* (Volume 2, Part 1, Figure 53; drawing by M. Schur; photograph by Dennis Seckler).

Page 77: **Top,** *Copper-alloy and glass jewelry/ornament from Burial 186* (Volume 2, Part 1, Figure 251; photograph by Jon Abbott). **Bottom left,** *Donut-shaped opaque yellow beads from Burial 226* (Volume 2, Part 1, Figure 243; photograph by Jon Abbott). **Bottom right,** *Cast silver pendant from Burial 254* (Volume 2, Part 1, Figure 252; photograph by Jon Abbott).

Page 78: *Burials 12 and 14* (Volume 2, Part 2: Page 17).

Page 79: *A woman and two children in a shared grave (Burials 142, 144, and 149)* (Volume 2, Part 1, Figure 86; photograph by Dennis Seckler).

Page 80: *Adult mortality: New York African Burial Ground and Trinity Church* (Volume 1, Part 1, Figure 52).

Page 81: *Bar graph representing sex and age at death for the 301 individuals observable for age and/or sex* (Volume 1, Part 1, Figure 26).

CHAPTER 6

Page 82: *Burial 122* (Volume 2, Part 2: Page 169; drawing by M. Schur).

Page 83: *Interment in the African Burial Ground* (Volume 3, Figure 20; illustration by Michael Colbert, 2004).

Page 84: **Left,** *Top of skull from Burial 323* (Volume 1, Part 1, Figure 5). **Right,** *Magnified saw marks on skull in Burial 323* (Volume 1, Part 1, Figure 6).

Page 85: **Top left,** *Turquoise enameled cuff link faces on copper-alloy backs, Burial 371* (Volume 2, Part 1, Figure 255; photograph by Jon Abbott). **Middle left,** *Detail of decorative motif on cuff-link faces from Burial 238* (Volume 2, Part 1, Figure 177; photograph by Jon Abbott). **Bottom left,** *Gilt, copper-alloy cuff links from Burial 158* (Volume 2, Part 1, Figure 155;

photograph by Jon Abbott). **Top right,** *Enamel jewelry/possible cuff-link or button face from Burial 211* (Volume 2, Part 1, Figure 214; photograph by Jon Abbott). **Middle right,** *Two pairs of copper-alloy cuff links were found near the wrists of the 40–50-year-old man in Burial 238* (Volume 2, Part 1, Figure 176; photograph by Jon Abbott). **Bottom right,** *Copper-alloy cuff link from Burial 392* (Volume 2, Part 1, Figure 214; photograph by Jon Abbott).

Page 86: **Top,** *Replicas of African Burial Ground pins* (Volume 2, Part 1, Figure 9; photograph by Rob Tucher). **Bottom,** *Pin with fabric from Burial 415* (Volume 2, Part 1, Figure 133; photograph by Jon Abbott).

Page 87: **Top left,** *Composite drawing of coffin handle* (Volume 2, Part 1, Figure 127; drawing by C. LaRoche and R. Schultz). **Top right,** *Burial 332 coffin lid, drawn as found during the excavation* (Volume 2, Part 1, Figure 128; drawing by M. Schur). **Bottom,** *Photograph of Burial 332 coffin lid decoration formed of iron tacks* (Volume 2, Part 1, Figure 95; photograph by Dennis Seckler).

Page 88: **Left,** *Plain, copper-alloy ring from "Burial 398"* (Volume 2, Part 1, Figure 248; photograph by Jon Abbott). **Top right,** *Plain, copper-alloy ring from Burial 71* (Volume 2, Part 1, Figure 246; photograph by Jon Abbott). **Middle right,** *Copper-alloy ring with glass insets from Burial 242* (Volume 2, Part 1, Figure 249; photograph by Jon Abbott). **Bottom right,** *Copper-alloy ring with glass insets from Burial 310* (Volume 2, Part 1, Figure 250; photograph by Jon Abbott).

Page 89: **Top row: Left,** *Buttons from Burial 6 associated with a man's coat or jacket* (Volume 2, Part 1, Figure 144; photograph by Jon Abbott). **Middle,** *Gilt, copper-alloy button from Burial 6* (Volume 2, Part 1, Figure 145; photograph by Jon Abbott). **Right,** *Detail of the disturbed Burial 181 with buttons in the pelvic area* (Volume 2, Part 1, Figure 159; drawing by M. Schur). **Middle row: Left,** *Detail of Burial 392 with buttons at knees and hips* (Volume 2, Part 1, Figure 206; drawing by M. Schur). **Middle,** *Bone buttons from Burial 392* (Volume 2, Part 1, Figure 207; photograph by Jon Abbott). **Right (clockwise from top left),** *Copper-alloy, with zinc and nickel, button from Burial 181* (Volume 2, Part 1, Figure 160; photograph by Jon Abbott). *Copper-alloy button, with bone back, Burial 181* (Volume 2, Part 1, Figure 164; photograph by Jon Abbott). *Copper-alloy button from Burial 181* (Volume 2, Part 1, Figure 162; photograph by Jon Abbott). **Bottom row: Left,** *Bone button from Burial 392* (Volume 2, Part 1, Figure 210; photograph by Jon Abbott). **Middle,** *Wool buttonhole from Burial 392* (Volume 2, Part 1, Figure 213; photograph by Jon Abbott). **Right,** *Bone and copper-alloy button from Burial 181* (Volume 2, Part 1, Figure 166; photograph by Jon Abbott).

Page 90: **Top,** *Opaque redwood on transparent apple-green core bead from Burial 107* (Volume 2, Part 1, Figure 234; photograph by Jon Abbott). **Middle,** *Translucent light gold-colored bead from Burial 340* (Volume 2, Part 1, Figure 236; photograph by Jon Abbott). **Bottom,** *Transparent light gray beads from Burial 428* (Volume 2, Part 1, Figure 239; photograph by Jon Abbott).

Page 91: **Top left,** *Opaque black bead from Burial 250* (Volume 2, Part 1, Figure 240; photograph by Jon Abbott). **Middle left,** *Tubular or cylindrical opaque white bead from Burial 434* (Volume 2, Part 1, Figure 242; photograph by Jon Abbott). **Bottom left,** *Barrel shaped, opaque black bead from Burial 340* (Volume 2, Part 1, Figure 241; photograph by

Jon Abbott). **Top right,** *Donut shaped to tubular opaque black bead from Burial 187* (Volume 2, Part 1, Figure 235; photograph by Jon Abbott). **Bottom right,** *Drawing of Burial 340 showing location of possible waist beads* (Volume 2, Part 1, Figure 229; redrawn by M. Schur from photocopy of original field drawing).

Page 92: Site location overlaid on the Ratzer Map (1767) (Volume 2, Part 1, Figure 34; Geography & Map Division, Library of Congress).

Page 93: **Left,** *Burial No. 335* (Volume 2, Part 2: Page 453; drawing by W. Williams). **Right,** *Detail of west-central portion of site plan showing all temporal groups* (Volume 2, Part 1, Figure 75).

Page 94: **Top,** *Detail of clay pipe bowl, showing IW mark (Burial 158 and drawing of bowl shape* (Volume 2, Part 1, Figure 268; photograph by Christopher R. DeCorse). **Middle,** *Photograph of clay pipe stem and bowl near the left forearm of Burial 165* (Volume 2, Part 1, Figure 269; photograph by Dennis Seckler). **Bottom,** *Clay pipe stem and bowl from Burial 165* (Volume 2, Part 1, Figure 270; photograph by Christopher R. DeCorse).

Page 95: **Top,** *Drawing of ceramic and copper-alloy sphere with band at the hip of the woman in Burial 375* (Volume 2, Part 1, Figure 66; drawing by M. Schur). **Bottom,** *Ceramic and copper-alloy sphere with band from Burial 375* (Volume 2, Part 1, Figure 271; photograph by Jon Abbott).

Page 96: **Top,** *Unused clay pipe from Burial 340* (Volume 2, Part 1, Figure 267; photograph by Jon Abbott). **Bottom,** *Photograph of stoneware vessel fragment from Burial 328* (Volume 2, Part 1, Figure 282; photograph by Dennis Seckler).

Page 97: **Top left,** *Copper-alloy coin from Burial 214* (Volume 2, Part 1, Figure 259; photograph by Jon Abbott). **Middle left,** *Knife handle from Burial 214* (Volume 2, Part 1, Figure 277; photograph by Jon Abbott). **Bottom left,** *Photograph of knife handle from the left forearm area of Burial 214* (Volume 2, Part 1, Figure 276; photograph by Dennis Seckler). **Top right,** *Drawing of Burial 214, showing artifact locations* (Volume 2, Part 1, Figure 275; drawing by M. Schur). **Bottom right,** *Copper-alloy button back from Burial 214* (Volume 2, Part 1, Figure 174; photograph by Jon Abbott).

Page 99: The African Methodist Episcopal Zion Church at Tenth and Bleecker Streets in New York City (The Picture Collection of the New York Public Library).

Page 101: **Top left,** *Coral from Burial 376* (Volume 2, Part 1, Figure 266; photograph by Dennis Seckler). **Middle left,** *Calcite-crystal cluster from Burial 55* (Volume 2, Part 1, Figure 279; photograph by Jon Abbott). **Bottom left,** *Glass sphere from Burial 410* (Volume 2, Part 1, Figure 274; photograph by Jon Abbott). **Top right,** *Mica schist disk from Burial 135* (Volume 2, Part 1, Figure 281; photograph by Jon Abbott). **Bottom right,** *Rose quartz disk from Burial 289* (Volume 2, Part 1, Figure 280; photograph by Jon Abbott).

CHAPTER 7

Page 102: One version of the West African Sankofa symbol (Volume 2, Part 1, Figure 286).

Page 103: Site location overlaid on the Maerschalk Plan (Volume 2, Part 1, Figure 33; Geography & Map Division, Library of Congress).

Page 104: Wooden coffins, hand-carved in Ghana, held the ancestors' remains for reburial at the New York African Burial Ground (Volume 2, Part 1: Epilogue; photograph by Anne and Jon Abbott).

Page 105: Mother Delois Blakely heads the procession of the coffins from Wall Street to the African Burial Ground (Volume 2, Part 1: Epilogue; photograph by Sherrill D. Wilson).

Page 107: African Burial Ground Memorial (courtesy U.S. General Services Administration, Carol M. Highsmith Photography, Inc.).

Page 109: Unearthed (courtesy U.S. General Services Administration).

$\mathcal{J}$NDEX

trade in goods, 16, 20, 52, 57, 58. *See also* fur trade; provisions trade

transatlantic slave trade. *See* trade in enslaved Africans

transfer of remains to Howard University. *See* Howard University: transfer of remains to

Trinity Church (Anglican), 40f

    attendance by Africans, 42

    ban on African burials within cemetery of, 40

    establishment of a burial ground for Africans, 42

    records of European deaths, 78, 80

23rd Street, 18

290 Broadway, 2, 6, 36, 38

typhoid, 74

Unearthed, 109f

United States, 16, 28, 34, 48, 50, 52, 95, 98, 106, 108

United States Congress, 6, 32

University of Notre Dame, 45f

U.S. Army Corps of Engineers, 104

Van Angola, Anthony (father), 35

Van Angola, Anthony (son), 35

Van Angola, Catalina, 35

Van Angola/d'Angola, Lucie, 35

Van Borsum, Cornelis, 19f

Van Borsum Patent, 36f, 38, 38f, 42, 92f

Vantilborough, Peter, 28

Van Zandt, John, 24

Varick Street, 19

Venice, 90

Vincent, Francis, 66

Vingboons, Johannes, 17f

violence, evidence of at the New York African Burial Ground, 26, 26f, 27f. *See also* fractures

violence against enslaved Africans, 24, 26, 27f, 64, 80. *See also* fractures

violence against enslavers, 28, 30

vitamin deficiency, 70, 72

Von Cortlandt, Jacobus, 22, 66

waist beads. *See under* beads

Walloons, 14

Wall Street, 40f, 104, 105f

wards, 64, 92f. *See also* Dock Ward; East Ward; South Ward; Bowery Ward; Haarlem Ward

Washington, D.C., 5f, 6, 104

Washington Monument, 6

Washington Square

    potter's field, as a burial site for Africans, 42

Washington Square Park, 19

West Africa, 20, 47, 49f, 50f, 51f, 54, 56, 58, 84, 94

West Central Africa, 16, 50f, 54, 56, 58, 94

West Fourth Street, 42

West Ward, 21f

"Whipper of slaves," 22

whooping cough, 74

William Street, 34

Wilson, Sherrill D., 8

W. Montague Cobb Laboratory, 106

W. Montague Cobb Skeletal Collection, 4

World Trade Center, 8

worms, 72

yaws, 74

yellow fever, 42, 74

Yorubaland, 100